Alice

Coleonyx variegatus

LIZARDS
KW-196

Photographers: William B. Allen Jr., Dr. Herbert R. Axelrod, Bertrand E. Baur, Horst Bielfeld, J. Bridges, Dr. Guido Dingerkus, P. v.d. Elzen (courtesy D. Terver, Nancy Aquarium, France), Isabelle Francais, Michael Gilroy, H. Hansen, Burkhard Kahl, W. Kastle, Alex Kerstitch, Knaack, J.K. Langhammer, Ken Lucas (Steinhart Aquarium), David R. Moenich, Aaron Norman, Elaine Radford, Ivan Sazima, R. Zukal.

Title page: A green spiny lizard, *Sceloporus malachitus*.

Acknowledgments: Special thanks to Elmer and Gary Knabe, owners of Elmer's Aquarium and Pet Center, Monroeville, PA, for lizard specimens they provided for photography. Many thanks to Lewis Bromer, Dave Grainy, Darryl Lott, Gary Myers, and Paula Reiss. Also, thanks to Edward and Linda Szalankiewicz.

Dedication: To my parents and family

© **Copyright 1990 by T.F.H. Publications, Inc.**

Distributed in the UNITED STATES by T.F.H. Publications, Inc., One T.F.H. Plaza, Neptune City, NJ 07753; in CANADA to the Pet Trade by H & L Pet Supplies Inc., 27 Kingston Crescent, Kitchener, Ontario N2B 2T6; Rolf C. Hagen Ltd., 3225 Sartelon Street, Montreal 382 Quebec; in CANADA to the Book Trade by Macmillan of Canada (A Division of Canada Publishing Corporation), 164 Commander Boulevard, Agincourt, Ontario M1S 3C7; in ENGLAND by T.F.H. Publications Limited, Cliveden House/Priors Way/Bray, Maidenhead, Berkshire SL6 2HP, England; in AUSTRALIA AND THE SOUTH PACIFIC by T.F.H. (Australia) Pty. Ltd., Box 149, Brookvale 2100 N.S.W., Australia; in NEW ZEALAND by Ross Haines & Son, Ltd., 82 D Elizabeth Knox Place, Panmure, Auckland, New Zealand; in the PHILIPPINES by Bio-Research, 5 Lippay Street, San Lorenzo Village, Makati Rizal; in SOUTH AFRICA by Multipet Pty. Ltd., Box 235 New Germany, South Africa 3620. Published by T.F.H. Publications, Inc. Manufactured in the United States of America by T.F.H. Publications, Inc.

LIZARDS

David R. Moenich

Contents

Opposite: *A green anole (*Anolis carolinensis*)*.

Preface

Lizards are cold-blooded vertebrates that are placed in the class Reptilia (reptiles). The classification of lizards is detailed further by their inclusion in the order Squamata; snakes also belong to this order. Sauria, a suborder, is reserved exclusively for lizards and comprises some 19 families. Within these 19 families are approximately 300 genera of lizards that collectively contain somewhere around 3000 species plus hundreds of additional subspecies.

The natural distribution of lizard species is almost worldwide. They are most plentiful in warm climates, although one species, *Lacerta vivipara*, is known to be indigenous as far north as just within the Arctic Circle.

The scientific names of lizards are printed in italic type, with the genus first (with an

Below: The viviparous lizard (Lacerta vivipara) *can be found in certain parts of Siberia.* *Opposite:* Knight anole (Anolis equestris).

The collared lizard (Crotaphytus collaris) is a member of the family Iguanidae and subfamily Sceloporinae.

initial capital letter) and the species name second. Many lizards that are popular among amateur herpetologists can be found listed under their respective climatic zone sections of this book. Many species and even entire families of lizards have been excluded from the main focus of this text due to undesirable traits of the lizards or lack of retail availability of specimens. The limbless lizards, for instance, have not been included in this book. These include the following families— Anelytropsidae, Anniellidae, Dibamidae, Feylinidae, and Pygopodidae. The Anguidae, which contains only some species that are limbless, has also been left out. Other families of lizards that have been excluded are Lanthanotidae and Xenosauridae (both rare), Xantusiidae (nocturnal), and Helodermatidae (poisonous).

Families of lizards that are represented in this book include Agamidae, Chamaeleontidae, Cordylidae, Gekkonidae, Iguanidae, Lacertidae, Scincidae, Teiidae, and Varanidae. These families provide over 95% of all lizards regularly sold through commercial channels.

Maintenance of proper conditions in indoor enclosures for lizards, with emphasis placed on climatic control and lizard nutrition, is the main concern of this book. Outdoor cages usually can be used only as temporary seasonal facilities in many climates that are temperate or cooler. Certain species of lizards can be permanently housed outdoors if they are indigenous to the area where they are being kept. However, this seems to be a futile arrangement if the lizards can readily be observed in their natural environment.

The care of lizards, as well as the care of all reptiles, presents a certain challege in regard to the duplication of the specimen's natural habitat. Most pets, with the exception of tropical fishes, demand far less exacting environmental conditions.

It might appear that people who are interested in keeping such exotic animals are just as fascinated by trying to reproduce the total atmosphere of the creature's natural habitat. An attempt to simulate any type of naturally occurring climatic environment, while continually meeting the

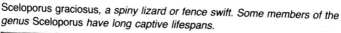

Sceloporus graciosus, a spiny lizard or fence swift. Some members of the genus Sceloporus have long captive lifespans.

needs of all the flora and fauna contained therein, can in many circumstances become quite a difficult task. The time, effort, and money invested in such a project most likely reflect the consequences that follow.

The author makes no promises in regard to the achievement of success by anyone who chooses to follow the suggestions that are given in this book. Much scientific information is still needed in the areas of reptilian biology, behavior, and environmental requirements of captive lizards. However, this text does constitute what the author believes to be the specifics of successful lizard-keeping. It is hoped that anyone who reads this book will benefit from the information presented here.

*Below: A pair of red-sided curly-tailed lizards (*Leiocephalus schreibersi*). **Opposite:** Headstudy of a common tegu (*Tupinambis teguixin*) and a savannah monitor (*Varanus exanthematicus*), bottom.*

Lizards in General

All lizards have a heart that contains three chambers, one incompletely divided ventricle and two complete auricles. The physical characteristics and oddities of individual species vary significantly. Although all species have skin that is composed of dry scales, some lizards have rough-textured skin while others are smooth. All lizards have teeth, but the sizes and types vary. Virtually all of these animals possess claws, and most of them have keen, well-developed eyes. Most species have eyelids that move to cover or expose the eye; others lack eyelids but are capable of cleaning their eyes with their tongues. Many of these creatures have forked tongues, and certain species have extremely long tongues that they project and retract at will (used for obtaining insects).

Lizards molt (shed, slough) their skin periodically. Most lizards have an acute sense of hearing. Certain lizards have prehensile tails that can be partially or completely regenerated. Most of these animals are diurnal (day-active) and oviparous (egg-layers); some are nocturnal (night-active) and/or viviparous (live-bearers).

Some species are endowed with suction-cup–like pads on

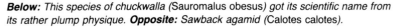

Below: This species of chuckwalla (Sauromalus obesus) *got its scientific name from its rather plump physique.* **Opposite:** Sawback agamid (Calotes calotes).

12

their feet that enable them to walk upside-down on a ceiling. Most lizards have four usable feet, but others lack feet entirely. Certain species are able to drastically change the color of their skin. The Jacobson's organ, which is located in the roof of the lizard's mouth, is very sensitive to chemicals in many species and aids the sense of smell.

Many lizards are insectivorous (insect-eaters); some are carnivorous (meat-eaters). A few species are

*A juvenile Chinese water dragon (*Physignathus cocincinus*) with a skink. Members of the genus* Physignathus *have strong teeth and jaws, and most are omnivorous.*

Jackson's chameleon (Chamaeleo jacksonii). This species is also called the three-horned chameleon.

entirely herbivorous (plant-eaters), and many species are omnivorous (anything-eaters). There are temperate, tropical, and desert lizards. Certain species can withstand high temperatures of 110° to 115°F (43–46°C), although exposing any lizard specimen to such an extreme level of heat certainly is not recommended. Direct continued exposure to sunlight without access to shade will kill any lizard. At least one species has a range that extends into a subarctic climate zone, but this lacertid spends a great deal of its life in hibernation.

Many lizards are primarily arboreal (tree-dwellers); others are mainly terrestrial (ground-dwellers). Certain species are semi-aquatic.

Many lizards are adorned with unique appendages, i.e., dewlaps, head crests, horns, fin-like dorsal crests, and enlarged or protruding scales or spines. Certain species can vocalize a screeching sound. Two species can inflict a venomous bite. Many lizard species possess a parietal or "third eye" that is located on the top of the lizard's head behind the eye region. There is

much speculation concerning the true function of this structure, which often is not very light-sensitive and probably serves more to regulate hormonal secretion than to see.

Lizards as pets leave much to be desired in the lovable and huggable department. They do not return affectionate emotions and are strictly instinctual in their behavior. The appeal of lizards to pet keepers most likely hinges on the animals' appearance and mannerisms. These are their only rational redeeming qualities. Their somewhat exotic demeanor might bring to mind thoughts of a tropical paradise somewhere far away in time.

Opposite: Madagascar day gecko *(*Phelsuma madagascariensis*). **Below:** A marine iguana (Amblyrhynchus cristatus). Marine iguanas are found on the Galapagos Islands; they are considered endangered and are not suitable for the terrarium.*

Terrarium Care

The most suitable and probably the most frequently used indoor enclosure in which lizards are housed is the all-glass aquarium. The smaller tanks are relatively inexpensive, but the larger, more costly sizes are available in many more different styles. With a little creative imagination this type of terrarium can be beautifully landscaped with an arrangement of rocks, driftwood, and plants. Large indoor showcases designed for plants might be an ideal situation to house certain species of lizards. In certain models the soil is heated by coils controlled by a thermostat, but many of these units are very costly.

A cage of appropriate size offers an option in the provision of both indoor and outdoor lizard housing. It is best to avoid the use of wire mesh screen when constructing the walls of the cage. Clear plastic panels can be used in place of metal screen if the cage is to be used indoors. Cages that are placed in a sunny location outdoors will require walls that allow ventilation. Since outdoor cages usually are used only as temporary housing, some type of screen, whether plastic or metal, is satisfactory. The use of abrasive screen material is discouraged due to abrasions that can result to the lizard, especially on the nose, if the specimen should attempt to escape through the woven metal walls. The size and shape of the cage are limited only by the builder's ability and bank account.

All lizards require adequate space for climbing and crawling; lack of exercise can cause atrophy of the lizard's muscle tissue. Many species of lizards are active and swift runners. If the area allotted to such a specimen is spacious enough to allow the lizard to run, the animal should feel secure enough in its captive environment to exhibit its natural behavior and disposition.

A source of heat must be available to the lizard during the daylight hours, as well as throughout the night if evening

Opposite: A green anole (Anolis carolinensis). This popular species likes warmth and relatively high humidity in its terrarium.

temperatures fall below 68–70°F (20–21°C). Lighting can be used as a means of generating heat, although this method is not applicable at night. When heating the habitat with lamps (incandescent bulbs deliver a much higher degree of heat than fluorescent tubes) a possible source of trouble can be created unless safety is considered first. Light bulbs and reflectors can become very hot to the touch. Lighting fixtures should be placed well out of the reach of children, as well as the lizards. High-wattage bulbs are potential fire hazards, especially when left on for a long time or when they are close to combustible materials.

Although the use of fluorescent lighting does not provide the amount of heat required for warming the lizard's environment, it does have at least one advantage. This beneficial feature is the option of using tubes that produce either a wide

Driftwood, often used as a terrarium furnishing, must come from a safe source—don't use it if you can't be sure that it is free from toxic chemicals.

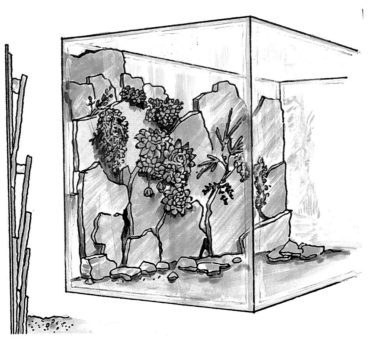

Attaching non-sedimentary rocks to the side of the terrarium is one way to add interest to a lizard's surroundings.

spectrum of light waves or illumination that focuses on the blue and/or red wavelengths. With the use of these tubes the lizards can be provided with a source of light that closely resembles natural sunlight.

Subjecting a lizard to the radiation of lighting devices that are designed for tanning purposes is taking an unnecessary risk with the health of the animal; prolonged exposure to such radiation can cause serious damage to the lizard.

An alternative method of providing lizards with heat is the use of one of the heat source elements commercially available for terraria. Certain types are fashioned in the likeness of a rock formation. This method of "dark" heating by "hot rocks" is especially useful for providing heat

*Chinese water dragon (*Physignathus cocincinus*). Rocks, plants, and tree limbs add interest to the terrarium set-up, but they must not overcrowd the lizard's habitat.*

throughout the night. During the daylight hours the radiation of heat from a light source, which enables the lizard to bask, is the preferred method.

When light bulbs are used in conjunction with "hot rocks" a wider variety of temperatures becomes available to the lizard. The heating "rock" can be positioned on the floor and strategically placed in the lizard's environment. The specimen then has the option of climbing onto the device, where it can regulate its body temperature in much the same manner as it would by lying on a warm rock. For fear of the obvious hazards of electricity, these devices as well as all other electrical equipment should never be exposed to wetness unless it can be guaranteed that the unit in question is waterproof.

Humidity requirements for lizards vary from species to species, depending on the climate they come from. A climate is comprised of many different elements, including: mean annual temperature; precipitation; relative humidity; amount of sunshine/cloudiness; and wind direction and

Common green iguana (Iguana iguana). If you use electrical devices, be sure to place water dishes well away from them.

velocity. Wind is probably rarely considered when deciding the possible environmental conditions in which to place an individual lizard specimen, and although the presence or absence of wind is probably not a crucial factor in successfully maintaining lizards, it seems appropriate that any environmental condition that can be duplicated in the captive habitat of any animal should be attempted.

Adequate air circulation certainly is necessary in any enclosed lizard habitat to prevent air stagnation, and in the case of tropical rain-forest environments, to prevent the growth of molds and other fungi. An answer to the question of producing an air current within the lizard's habitat might be the placement

A variety of light bulbs suitable for use in the terrarium can be found at your local pet shop.

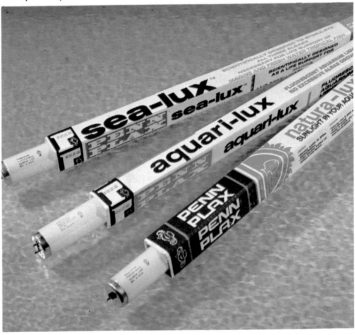

*A five-lined skink (*Eumeces fasciatus*). Some lizard species need to be provided with ample hiding places.*

of a small circular fan above the terrarium, with the top of the enclosure at least partially covered by a screen. If the inhabitants retreat when the fan is turned on, try locating the fan further away from the terrarium. As with all electrical appliances, never allow the fan to come into contact with water.

As far as providing heat and light are concerned, the available alternatives make it seem reasonable that daytime lighting using a mixture of suitable fluorescent tubes and incandescent bulbs rated at 60 watts or less is the safest and most efficient way of meeting these requirements.

Temperate and Subtropical Zones

TEMPERATE CLIMATE

The term "temperate" suggests that the weather conditions within this climate type are moderate in all ways. However, mean annual temperatures can vary significantly from region to region, and maximum high and low fluctuations in daily thermometer readings differ within each individual area.

Daytime high temperatures in summer months can register close to 100°F (38°C). This might well be accompanied by a relative humidity factor of nearly 100%. Such uncomfortable conditions are seldom found in tropical rain-forest climates of the world's jungles.

By contrast, winter temperatures are capable of dipping far below 0°F. Although relative humidity is much lower during the winter months, many areas that are defined as temperate zones receive heavy snowfalls. Average annual precipitation, both rain and snow, is approximately 20–40 inches (50–100 cm) in temperate climates.

A temperate climate prevails throughout the northeastern United States as far south as the border of Virginia and North Carolina. This temperate zone stretches west to approximately 100°W longitude. Much of Europe is also in a temperate climate, and many relatively smaller areas of this climate type are scattered throughout the world.

Considering the harsh extremes in temperature that must be endured by the indigenous reptiles, it seems reasonable that the number of lizard species is limited in these climatic regions, but certain skinks (Scincidae), lacertids (Lacertidae), and swifts (Iguanidae) are capable of thriving in such environments. These mainly terrestrial lizards must burrow into the earth or otherwise secure a location for hibernation when the cold winter months arrive. Overexposure to extreme heat is also life-threatening to these lizards.

SUBTROPICAL CLIMATE

A subtropical climate is, as the name implies, somewhat less than tropical. Although winters in these zones are much milder than those of temperate regions, frost is a possibility and extreme low temperatures can occasionally drop to $-5°F$ ($-21°C$).

It is impossible to keep more than one male wall lizard (Podarcis muralis) in a single terrarium, as they will fight each other to the death. It is, however, quite feasible to keep one male with two or three females.

Plastic plants may look artificial, but they can withstand the abuse dished out by active lizards and, more importantly, they are not likely to have been treated with toxic chemicals.

Normally, winter day temperatures average from 55 to 60°F (13–16°C), while night temperatures average from 35 to 45°F (2–8°C).

Summer months usually average from 75 to 80°F (24–27°C) during the day, and nighttime lows are ordinarily in the high 50s to the low 70s F (15–22°C). Extreme daytime highs can reach 110°F (43°C). Average summer humidity is approximately 70% to 80%. Average annual precipitation is 30 to 65 inches (76–165 cm).

Almost all of the southeastern United States below the border of Virginia and North Carolina is encompassed by a subtropical climate. This subtropical zone, like the temperate zone of the United States, reaches west to approximately 100°W longitude (extreme southern Florida is excluded from this climatic zone). Most of the West Coast of the United States has a subtropical climate, and much of southern Europe is subject to a subtropical clime that is sometimes referred to as a Mediterranean climate. Other areas with subtropical climate that are not as extensive can be found in extreme northern and southern Africa as well as eastern and southern Australia. In South America subtropical zones are located in part of southern Brazil, a section of northeastern Argentina, and all of Uruguay.

CLIMATE CONTROL AND ENVIRONMENT

Lizards that are native to temperate and subtropical climates usually can be kept under the same terrarium conditions. The naturally occurring excessive high and low temperatures and relative humidity can be eliminated within an indoor terrarium.

To prevent a lizard from going into a partial state of hibernation, which renders the reptile's stomach unable to digest food properly, the night temperature probably should not drop any lower than 68 to 70°F (20–21°C). Daytime highs that range from 70 to 85°F (21–30°C) will most often

*A western skink (*Eumeces skiltonianus*). In general, skinks should not be kept with other members of their species, since these lizards tend to be very aggressive among themselves.*

prove to be the ideal temperatures for most temperate and subtropical species.

Many species of lizards, regardless of climatic origin, will drink water from a bowl or other container. The provision of water can be as simple as the inclusion of a water dish or as complicated as the elaborate arrangement of a waterfall and its corresponding lagoon.

Drinking water, as well as water that is provided for the lizard to soak in, should always be clean. The bowl should be emptied and refilled daily. If chlorine in tap water is a concern, bottled mineral water is commercially available. Many lizards are good swimmers, but others are not so adept. To eliminate the threat of a fatal fall into a water dish, it is a good idea to place non-sedimentary rocks, such as red shale, in an arrangement that provides the lizard with ease of access both

into and out of the water. Either a drip system or the use of an air stone in conjunction with the water bowl will increase humidity as well as enable the lizard to find the water more easily. (Drip systems and air stone agitation of the water should be avoided in desert terrariums.)

Plastic plants can be used to decorate the terrarium environment, although they inspire nearly the same apathy in the viewer of such a habitat as do their sea-going counterparts that can be found in many uninteresting aquariums. Although plastic plants give the terrarium an unnatural "look," they do have their advantages. Many "species" of fake plants are tough enough to withstand the abuse that is sometimes dealt out by rambunctious lizards. Additionally, the probability that pesticides have been applied prior to purchase is extremely remote. Conversely, most real plants will probably harbor these toxic substances. It is advisable to thoroughly clean any plant that has been purchased from a source where pesticide contamination is a possibility, although all traces of the poisonous chemicals might not be

Opposite: A Jamaican giant anole (Anolis garmani). *Members of this species are forest dwellers.*

removable. This is a special concern when keeping herbivores and lizards that drink droplets of water from the leaves of plants.

When real plants are included in the environment it is suggested that they remain in individual pots. If the terrarium is a wood-framed cage, the use of a false bottom can be advantageous. Assuming that the bottom is constructed of plywood, it is fairly easy to locate the areas where the plants are to be positioned and cut out holes of appropriate sizes that will accommodate the corresponding plant pots. When the pots are arranged a suitable substrate can then be applied to cover their tops.

There are several types of natural-looking gravels that are manufactured primarily for use in freshwater tropical fish aquaria. These substrates are well-suited for use in terraria. A potting soil mixture can be used in place of gravel. Regardless of the medium that is used to cover the floor of the terrarium, cleanliness must be maintained, and periodic replacement of the gravel or soil is recommended. If a false bottom is in place, the substrate can be changed with

much less disturbance to the plants.

Decorations of the temperate/subtropical environment should reflect the natural habitat of the individual species. Terrestrial lizards should be provided with plenty of ground cover, such as horizontally positioned branches, pieces of tree bark, and rocks that are light enough for the animals to burrow under. Upright branches might also be included; even those lizards that are considered to be terrestrial will occasionally climb if they are furnished with the means to do so. Arboreal species can be afforded some ground cover in their environment, although the main concern is the provision of twigs, limbs, and branches that offer the lizards a variety of perches that are located at different distances from the overhead heat and light sources. Driftwood, although usually expensive, can be a very attractive addition to most terraria.

Whether the decor is comprised of branches, driftwood, or small and/or large stones and rocks, the safety of the inhabitants of the habitat should be considered. Rock formations and arrangements

*An Italian wall lizard (*Podarcis sicula*). This species is considered easy to keep in captivity since it is quite adaptable.*

of branches should be secured to prevent the specimens from being crushed by an unstable construction of scenery. Also check for sharp splinters and ends on branches, as well as unusually sharp edges on rocks and all other decor.

Plants that are most suited to the temperate/subtropical terrarium require a relative humidity factor of approximately 50% to 60%.

The lizards that inhabit this type of terrarium are normally exposed to much higher relative humidity readings during the summer months, but it is a difficult task to constantly provide the optimum conditions for both plants and lizards at the same time. However, to achieve a natural environment it seems necessary to include living plants of some kind.

*A desert spiny lizard (*Sceloporus magister*). As its name implies, this species enhabits deserts and semi-deserts.*

The spider plant, *Chlorophytum*, is a hardy plant that requires full sun; this plant might do well in a temperate/subtropical environment. Other possible candidates include *Cordyline*, *Setcreasea*, and *Yucca* plants. These are all plants that require full sun. *Yucca* has hazardous points at the ends of its leaves. Nevertheless, this plant makes a beautiful appearance in just about any location. Another drawback to yuccas is their inclination to demand cool temperatures during the winter months.

Stenotaphrum (St. Augustine's grass), which also requires full sun, might be grown successfully in the temperate/subtropical habitat. *Dracaena* and *Ficus* (fig) plants, which need plenty of light, should not be exposed to direct sunlight. There are many species of broad-leaved fig plants as well as certain species, such as *Ficus rubiginosa*, that are ivy-like in appearance.

Successful maintenance of plants in a terrarium environment depends on many different elements, including soil type, fertilization, watering, and special individual requirements.

It seems best that only organic fertilizers, such as cow manure, should be used in a

The spider plant (Chlorophytum bichetii), also known as the grass lily or bride's veil, is one of several plants that does well in a temperate/subtropical terrarium.

terrarium that contains lizards. Most other fertilizers will prove to be irritants to the eyes and mucous membranes of lizards; the skin might also become irritated. In severe cases certain fertilizers can cause the demise of these reptiles, especially if the plant food is ingested. Pesticides should never be applied in terrariums that are used for housing lizards.

The use of foliage plants in temperate/subtropical habitats provides the lizards with the option of retreating into the shade offered by the leafy vegetation. The provision of a shaded location is mandatory in all types of lizard environments. The lizards as well as the plants should do best with a day/night schedule of 12 to 16 hours of sunlight and eight to 12 hours of dark.

TEMPERATE AND SUBTROPICAL LIZARDS
Eastern Fence Swift (*Sceloporus undulatus*)
FAMILY: Iguanidae
LIFESTYLE: Arboreal/terrestrial; field and forest

*A five-lined skink (*Eumeces fasciatus*). Eumeces *species resemble members of the genus* Lacerta *except for their smoother skins and shorter limbs.*

*An eyed lizard (*Lacerta lepida*). Members of the genus* Lacerta *are notoriously good climbers; they should be provided with tree limbs and rocks in the terrarium.*

DIET: Mainly insectivorous or somewhat omnivorous
AVERAGE LENGTH: 10 inches (25 cm)
NATIVE CLIMATE: Temperate, subtropical, steppe, and desert
NATURAL DISTRIBUTION: Parts of the northeastern, southern, central, and southwestern United States

This lizard is indigenous to many areas of the United States. It is essential to discover the climatic region of its origin to assure proper environmental conditions for each individual specimen.

Eyed Lizard (*Lacerta lepida*)
FAMILY: Lacertidae
LIFESTYLE: Terrestrial/arboreal; mostly field-oriented (rocks); also climbs trees
DIET: Omnivorous
AVERAGE LENGTH: 24 inches (61 cm)

Above: Schneider's skink (Eumeces schneideri). *This species is also called the dotted or sand skink.* *Below:* A five-lined skink (Eumeces fasciatus) *with two tails. This lizard's second tail was probably grown, by regeneration, after damage to the original.*

NATIVE CLIMATE: Temperate and subtropical

NATURAL DISTRIBUTION: Europe, Asia Minor

This quick, sure-footed lizard is at home on the ground as well as in the trees. Its somewhat aggressive behavior and its feeding habits suggest that this species be housed only with lizards of similar size and temperament. Offer flowers, fruit, and green foliage in addition to insects and flesh.

Five-lined Skink (*Eumeces fasciatus*)

FAMILY: Scincidae

LIFESTYLE: Terrestrial

burrowers; primarily forest-oriented

DIET: Insectivorous

AVERAGE LENGTH: 7½ inches (19 cm)

NATIVE CLIMATE: Temperate and subtropical

NATURAL DISTRIBUTION: Eastern North America

The smooth-scaled five-lined skink has a detachable tail that can be regenerated when broken. Many species of skinks are easy to maintain in good health if they are properly cared for. Skinks usually are moderately priced and frequently available for retail purchase.

*A broad-headed skink (*Eumeces laticeps*). Members of this species occasionally climb trees.*

*A trio of green anoles (*Anolis carolinensis*). The anole in the center is molting—note how dull his shedding skin is when compared with the bright green hides of his companions.*

Green Anole (*Anolis carolinensis*)

FAMILY: Iguanidae
LIFESTYLE: Arboreal; forest-oriented
DIET: Insectivorous
AVERAGE LENGTH: 7 inches (18 cm)
NATIVE CLIMATE: Subtropical and savannah
NATURAL DISTRIBUTION: Southeastern United States

Often sold under the mistaken identity of "American chameleon," this anole is possibly the most widely known and most frequently purchased species of lizard in the United States. It is abundant in its native area and is therefore a relatively inexpensive lizard.

These lizards are capable of rapid color changes and are able to exhibit many shades of green and brown. The green anole is equipped with toe pads that enable it to climb vertically on glass walls. The male of the species is endowed with a red to orange dewlap that it often displays during territorial disputes and mating rituals.

Although readily available and relatively inexpensive, this iguanid usually lives only a short time in captivity—two years of terrarium life might be considered the maximum for many specimens. Perhaps this is the result of an inadequate reproduction of the lizard's natural diet in captive environments. In addition, when purchased these lizards are often fully mature adult specimens. Their life span in the wild might also be short.

Green Lizard (*Lacerta viridis*)
FAMILY: Lacertidae
LIFESTYLE: Arboreal/terrestrial; primarily field-oriented; also climbs trees
DIET: Omnivorous
AVERAGE LENGTH: 15 inches (37 cm)
NATIVE CLIMATE: Temperate and subtropical
NATURAL DISTRIBUTION: Europe, Asia Minor

The common green lizard might be thought of as Europe's answer to the green

*A green lizard (*Lacerta viridis*). During the mating season, males of this species develop blue throats.*

*The green lizard (*Lacerta viridis)*, also known as the emerald lizard, is relatively adaptable, does well in captivity and breeds easily.*

anole of North America. However, the green lizard is much larger and its diet is much different from that of the green anole.

Six-lined Racerunner (*Cnemidophorus sexlineatus*)
FAMILY: Teiidae
LIFESTYLE: Mainly terrestrial; primarily field-oriented (flat and rocky areas)
DIET: Mainly insectivorous and carnivorous, but also somewhat herbivorous
AVERAGE LENGTH: 11½ inches (29 cm)
NATIVE CLIMATE: Temperate, subtropical, and steppe
NATURAL DISTRIBUTION: Parts of northeastern, southeastern, and

central United States

These are fast-running lizards that would benefit from an extremely large captive environment. As with the eastern fence swift, the natural climatic zone of the individual should be identified. Reproduction in some southwestern United States relatives of these lizards achieved through parthenogenesis: the eggs are laid without prior fertilization and there appear to be only females in the species. This species reproduces normally, however.

Wall Lizard (*Podarcis muralis*)

FAMILY: Lacertidae
LIFESTYLE: Terrestrial/arboreal; primarily field-oriented
DIET: Insectivorous/herbivorous
AVERAGE LENGTH: 7 inches (18 cm)
NATIVE CLIMATE: Temperate and subtropical
NATURAL DISTRIBUTION: Europe; introduced but not well established in northeastern United States

These quick little lizards will sometimes accept plant foliage or leafy vegetables as part of their diet.

The dotted racerunner (Cnemidophorus lemniscatus) is somewhat larger than the six-lined racerunner, and its natural habitat ranges from Honduras to Guyana.

Tropical Zones

TROPICAL RAIN-FOREST CLIMATE

A tropical rain-forest climate is also known as a "wet tropical climate." This implies that the area tends to receive large amounts of rainfall. Many regions of tropical rain forest lack a dry season or at most only two months are dry. Average annual precipitation is 70 to over 100 inches (180–250 cm). Temperatures remain consistently high and there is no winter season. The mean annual temperature is 77 to 81°F (25–27°C). Daytime high temperatures range from 85°F (30°C) to the low 90s F (32–34°C).

The highest temperature measured at Santarem, Brazil, along the Amazon River in the Amazon Basin of South America, was 96°F (36°C). The lowest temperature recorded in this area was 65°F (18°C); this is just slightly below the usual tropical rain-forest nighttime lows of 68 to 75°F (20–24°C). Average humidity can be estimated at approximately 85% and above. Tropical rain-forest climates are located primarily within a range of 10° latitude poleward in both directions from the Equator.

Regions of the world that are influenced by the presence of a tropical rain-forest climate include: most of the eastern half of Central America; part of the northwestern coastline of South America; most of the western half of South America from 15°S latitude to 10°N latitude (this includes the Amazon Basin); the Congo Basin of Africa; a small section on the eastern coast of Africa; eastern Madagascar; all of Malaya; almost all of the Indonesian islands including Sumatra; New Guinea; the eastern Philippines; and parts of Southeast Asia.

TROPICAL SAVANNAH CLIMATE

The "wet-and-dry tropical climate" is sometimes referred to as a savannah climate due to the naturally occurring "savannah grasses" that are common throughout these regions. Savannah climates occur mainly between 20°N and S latitude.

Mean annual temperature for this type of climate is at least

*Opposite: Tropical lizards, like the Chinese water dragon (*Physignathus cocincinus*), require warm temperatures and ample humidity.*

44

Helmeted iguana (Corytophanes cristatus). *Males of this species are recognizable by the large helmet.*

70°F (21°C). Savannah climates lack a winter, but distinct seasons are determined by temperature and amount of precipitation. The "cool/dry season" produces daytime high temperatures of 80 to 90°F (27–32°C), while nighttime lows of 70 to slightly less than 60°F (21–15°C) are common. Relative humidity during this season is lower than that of the "wet season" that precedes it. The "cool/dry season" eventually gives way to the "hot/dry season," which brings temperatures of 90 to over 100°F (32–38°C) for daytime highs. The "hot/dry season" ends as the "wet season" gets under way. "Wet season" temperatures and humidity factors can be compared to those of the tropical rain-forest climate. The average annual precipitation of the tropical savannah climate is 40 to 60 inches (102–152 cm).

Tropical savannah climate is represented on the United States mainland only by extreme southern Florida, including the Florida Keys.

The Bahamas, Cuba, and the Caribbean islands also exhibit the savannah climate. Other areas of the world that exhibit this climate type are as follows: the western half of Central America; most of the eastern half of South America; parts of northern South America; much of Africa from the Tropic of Capricorn to approximately 13°N latitude; western and central Madagascar; much of

*Common green iguanas (*Iguana iguana*) are among the most popular of the tropical lizards that can be kept in captivity.*

Southeast Asia; parts of Indonesia and the Philippines; and northern Australia.

CLIMATE CONTROL AND ENVIRONMENT

Tropical lizards are undoubtedly the most beautifully colored lizards in the world. Many tropical species display interesting behaviors. Certain species are renowned just for their exotic appearance. Although many tropical lizards are plentiful in their natural environment, most species are quite expensive when purchased from a retail pet store. The introduction to the market of the common green iguana is most likely responsible for stirring up interest in tropical lizards as pets.

Lizards that are indigenous to either of the two tropical climates can in most cases be maintained in the same type of terrarium setting. A tropical rain-forest habitat, which is jungle-like in appearance, provides the medium for a personal creative touch to be applied. The savannah climate occurs naturally in regions where expansive fields might be interrupted by a limited number of trees.

The tropical rain forest can be comprised of five tiers or levels of vegetation, the uppermost ceiling sometimes higher than 100 feet (30 m). The intense sunlight beats down directly upon the tops of these tall trees. Underneath the ceiling are additional tiers of trees, each level progressively closer to the ground than the one before it. When the ceiling is considered as the first tier, the fourth tier is comprised of trees that average 60 feet (18m) or less in height. The bottom level, the fifth tier, contains saplings, low-growing palms, shrubs, and herbs among the thick vegetation.

The varying degrees of sunlight that penetrate the successive levels of the rain forest must provide drastic differences in temperature from sheltered ground level to open "rooftop" level. To provide the optimum climatic conditions within a tropical habitat, it seems important to ensure the presence of a varied range of suitable temperatures.

Opposite: A spiny-tailed iguana (Ctenosaura *sp.) climbing a tree in its native Costa Rica.*

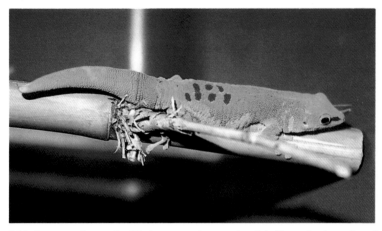

*A Madagascar day gecko (*Phelsuma madagascariensis*). Several subspecies of this lizard have been hybridized in captivity.*

Daytime highs are probably best kept between 75 and 90°F (24–32°C) when an attempt is made to duplicate a tropical environment. Nighttime temperatures should not drop below 68°F (20°C). Humidity is high in the tropical environment; 80 to 90% relative humidity is required to simulate this type of habitat. Unless the individual maintaining the habitat lives in a tropical climate, the humidity factor that is necessary will have to be synthetically produced. This task is fairly easy in the confines of an all-glass terrarium.

To increase humidity, increase the presence of water. The larger the surface area of the water bowl or container, the more humid the enclosed environment will become due to evaporation from the surface of the water. The use of an air stone in the water will increase humidity if the bubbles are moving briskly enough to distribute droplets of water erratically in the vicinity of the water hole. A drip system will also provide humidity in the same manner as an air stone. Watering the terrarium plants at their bases, which should be enclosed in plant pots, as well as spraying the foliage with water will create a higher humidity reading.

The top of the terrarium should be partially covered by

clear glass or clear hard plastic. The edges of this cover should be void of sharp surfaces, and the cover itself should be securely fastened to the top of the terrarium to ensure that injuries will not be inflicted on the inhabitants due to a cover that slips from its intended position. The cover is used to keep the humidity inside the terrarium, but the environment must be ventilated somewhat to discourage the growth of molds and other fungi. A screen can be placed over the portion of the terrarium top that is not covered by the glass or plastic. The use of a small fan might provide needed ventilation without greatly decreasing the humidity factor when the fan is used

Low-wattage aquarium heaters can be used successfully in tropical terrariums. Your local pet shop will have a wide selection from which to choose.

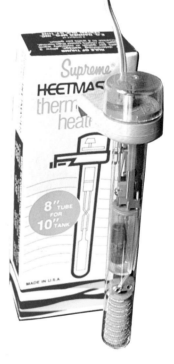

intelligently and applied at a low velocity.

A method that provides heat and humidity simultaneously is the practice of heating water in a separate gallon jar or small aquarium with the use of a low-wattage aquarium heater. This technique, which is simple in theory and execution, has a few drawbacks. The water level must be checked frequently due to evaporation, which is the basic principle on which the contraption works, providing warm moisture to the air. It is imperative to maintain the water level at the proper height to avoid creating a possible electrical fire hazard. Additionally, if the heating tube should crack, the water might become electrified. The combination of water and electricity can be fatal to humans as well as lizards.

If the heating jar is accessible to the lizards it is almost certain that the specimens will occasionally defecate into the jar. This necessitates the removal, cleaning, and replacement of the entire assembly. When constructing the homemade heater it is necessary to secure a piece of snug-fitting screen to the top of the container. This will permit heat and moisture to be emitted from the jar and should prevent the animals that inhabit the environment from entering the jar.

This method of supplying heat and humidity to the terrarium environment is not recommended by the author. It has only been mentioned here in the hopes that those who employ this technique will put safety first. When this method is used it is important to regulate the water at a warm, not hot, temperature.

High humidity most likely allows the lizards to absorb some moisture through their skin. This might enable them to molt with less difficulty. Regardless of the humidity factor, tropical lizards should be supplied with an ample amount of water to drink and soak in at their discretion. On hot and/or dry days most of these species would probably benefit from a room-temperature shower dispensed from a plant-spraying device

Opposite: A red-sided curly-tailed lizard (Leiocephalus schreibersi). Members of this species are also known as Haitian curly-tailed lizards.

A common green iguana (Iguana iguana). Most lizards dislike being handled, but handling is sometimes necessary. Have your pet dealer or an experienced hobbyist show you the proper way to hold your pet.

that is devoid of even the slightest trace of chemicals or fertilizers that might be used for treating or feeding plants.

Although the presence of moisture (in the air) and water (for drinking and soaking) is a crucial environmental requirement that should be provided in the tropical habitat, an overall wet or damp condition that could lead to skin infection and/or overall deterioration of health in the lizard must be avoided.

A rain-forest aqua-terrarium that is suitable for certain species of tropical lizards can be lavishly decorated.

Although the procedure of designing the habitat, as well as the continued maintenance that is required to ensure the proper ecological balance and functionality of the environment, can be an expensive and time-consuming venture, it might also be a very rewarding accomplishment to achieve success after such an investment.

In all aqua-terraria that support animal or plant life the water must be filtered. Biological filtration with the use of an undergravel filter should be employed. The depth of the water ideally should be 12 inches (30 cm) or more. Water temperature might best be kept at approximately 80°F (27°C). The addition of live aquatic plants is recommended. Small fishes that are temperature-compatible and lizard-compatible might be added; the addition of piranhas in this situation would have to be considered a mistake.

Although the inclusion of a sizable volume of water is essential for certain species of tropical lizards, i.e., water dragons, their environment must allow an adequate portion of dry terrain that enables the lizards to climb and crawl freely. Branches that overhang the water are a necessity. Easy access both in and out of the water must be provided.

A waterfall can be incorporated into the aqua-terrarium. A submersible water pump of the type used in small goldfish ponds might be applicable to this situation. The

pump must be positioned in a location that is inaccessible to the lizards both above and below the waterline. If placed in the bottom rear corner of the aqua-terrarium, an extension tube can be attached to the outflow port of the pump. The tube can then be positioned in

*A golddust day gecko (*Phelsuma laticauda*). The common name of this species comes from its pattern of small gold dots.*

the upper rear corner and can be used as a downspout.

An arrangement of rocks in a fashion that resembles a natural waterfall can be assembled to conceal the true identity of the water source. In the aqua-terrarium habitat the most functional substrate is aquarium gravel. Any decor that is suitable for tropical fish should be safe to use in the aqua-terrarium. This includes non-sedimentary rocks and driftwood, as well as numerous other decorations that are man-made.

Substrates and decors that are applicable to the "dry" tropical environment mirror the recommendations that were · given for temperate/subtropical habitats. Plants can be added to the aqua-terrarium if the obvious difficulties of placement as well as concealment of the plant pots can be overcome. Air plants (bromeliads) might be welcome additions to such an arrangement.

There are many species of plants that might be included in the tropical terrarium. These

Angel's wings (Caladium) *are suitable for the tropical terrarium but require indirect sunlight.*

The conehead *(*Laemanctus longipes*) is an omnivore, consuming mass quantities of different types of food.*

plants require approximately the same temperature and relative humidity factors as the tropical lizards that might share the environment. Two plants that require full sun are *Coleus* (flame nettle) and *Musa* (banana). Banana plants are attractive and appropriate when small, but if properly cared for these plants might outgrow the habitat.

Plants that are suitable for use in tropical lizard environments usually are cultivated for their lush foliage. Genera that require abundant indirect sunlight include *Alloplectus, Alocasia,*

Caladium (angel's wings), *Calathea, Ctenanthe, Maranta* (prayer plant), and *Pellonia.*

The pineapple plant (*Ananas*) can be grown from the fruit. The top section of the fruit, which contains the leaves, should be removed and potted after the bit of fruit remaining at the bottom of the cutting has dried for several days. The avocado (*Persea*) can be germinated in water. To do this, insert several toothpicks into the pit, place the pit in a glass or jar, and add water. The toothpicks are used to suspend the pit from the top of the container.

Approximately 1 inch (2.5 cm) of the pit should be submerged. It is time to pot the pit when many roots are present. The avocado and pineapple plants require full sunlight and are suitable plants to include in a tropical terrarium.

The aforementioned plants represent only a sample of the live plants that might be successfully maintained in a tropical habitat. The possibility of failure or success in an attempt to establish a well-balanced environment for lizards and live plants is probably determined by many factors. The individual who has the aid of a "green thumb" will most likely be a step ahead of the game.

Certain species of plants are poisonous and should not be included in a terrarium that houses lizards. *Senecio macroglossus*, an ivy-like tropical plant, is a poisonous species. Likewise, *Philodendron* is a toxic plant. Certain plants require specific care. The tropical zebra arrowroot, *Calathea*, although suitable for the terrarium throughout most of the year, tends to prefer a slightly cooler temperature during the winter. Recommendations

concerning plant fertilizers and pesticides, as well as a suitable day/night schedule and the provision of a shaded area within the tropical terrarium, parallel the suggestions given for temperate/subtropical habitats.

From a romantic point of view, a rain-forest habitat simulated within the confines of a terrarium seems to be the most beneficial environment that can be provided for tropical lizards. This type of environment also offers the most appealing approach to the keeper. In practice, however, the scenic beauty of even the best-designed terrarium maintained by the average amateur herpetologist might be demolished by the ever-increasing size and activity of the rapidly growing larger species of lizards. A walk-in greenhouse or similar structure is then necessary if the lizard is to be provided with a jungle-like environment. Hatchling lizards of large

Opposite: A helmeted chameleon (Chamaeleo hoehneli). This chameleon adapts well to captivity—it is not as nervous as other members of its genus.

tropical species might be housed in rain-forest terraria without much noticeable decline of the flora and decor.

TROPICAL LIZARDS
Brown Basilisk (*Basiliscus basiliscus*)
FAMILY: Iguanidae
LIFESTYLE: Mostly arboreal/also terrestrial; forest
DIET: Mainly carnivorous
AVERAGE LENGTH: 27 inches (68 cm)
NATIVE CLIMATE: Savannah, tropical rain forest
NATURAL DISTRIBUTION: Central America

This lizard is noted for its appearance as well as its behavior. The male is adorned with a unique head crest and an unusual fin-like dorsal ridge. The basilisk is capable of running a short distance on its hind legs atop the surface of water; it is also able to run bipedally on land.

Chinese Water Dragon (*Physignathus cocincinus*)
FAMILY: Agamidae
LIFESTYLE: Arboreal/semi-aquatic; forest
DIET: Omnivorous
AVERAGE LENGTH: 27 inches (68 cm)
NATIVE CLIMATE: Savannah, tropical rain forest

*The brown basilisk (*Basiliscus basiliscus*) is one of the lizards that should occasionally receive ultraviolet radiation.*

*An adult Chinese water dragon (*Physignathus cocincinus*). In the wild, this species is omnivorous, subsisting on fish, tadpoles, and water beetles.*

NATURAL DISTRIBUTION: Southeast Asia

These lizards, like the basilisks, use their hind legs to run in an upright position. Hatchlings of this species are very similar in appearance to those of *Iguana iguana*, the common green iguana.

Common Green Iguana (*Iguana iguana*)
FAMILY: Iguanidae
LIFESTYLE: Arboreal/somewhat terrestrial; forest
DIET: Hatchlings and juveniles mainly insectivorous; adults mainly herbivorous
AVERAGE LENGTH: 5 feet (152 cm)
NATIVE CLIMATE: Savannah, tropical rain forest
NATURAL DISTRIBUTION: Central and South America

For information concerning this species consult the "Iguana Primer" chapter.

Tegus (*Tupinambis* spp.)
FAMILY: Teiidae
LIFESTYLE: Terrestrial; forest
DIET: Omnivorous

*A common tegu (*Tupinambis teguixin*). This lizard is also known as the gold or black tegu. Due to its large adult size, this species requires a spacious terrarium.*

AVERAGE LENGTH: 3½ feet (107 cm)

NATIVE CLIMATE: Tropical rain forest, savannah

NATURAL DISTRIBUTION: South America

Two species of lizard are called tegus. The gold or black tegu (*Tupinambis teguixin*) and its racial variation (*Tupinambis t. nigropunctatus*) are more frequently available for retail purchase than the red tegu (*Tupinambis rufescens*). Care of these taxa is similar. Large specimens are capable of devouring chickens.

Helmeted Iguana (*Corytophanes cristatus*)

FAMILY: Iguanidae

LIFESTYLE: Arboreal; forest

DIET: Insectivorous and carnivorous

AVERAGE LENGTH: 14 inches (35 cm)

NATIVE CLIMATE: Savannah, tropical rain forest

NATURAL DISTRIBUTION: Central America

An extremely interesting lizard with an unusual appearance, this iguanid is rather difficult to maintain in good health if environmental and dietary conditions are less than superior.

Horned Mountain Dragon (*Acanthosaura crucigera*)
FAMILY: Agamidae
LIFESTYLE: Terrestrial and somewhat arboreal; forest
DIET: Insectivorous
AVERAGE LENGTH: 11 inches (28 cm)
NATIVE CLIMATE: Savannah, tropical rain forest
NATURAL DISTRIBUTION: Southeast Asia, Malaya, and Sumatra

The horned mountain dragon is virtually unique in its natural dietary preference for grubs and earthworms. This indicates that the species spends a good deal of time on or near the ground where temperatures in a lush tropical rain forest are not nearly as high as in the sun-drenched areas of these regions.

Jackson's Chameleon (*Chamaeleo jacksonii*)
FAMILY: Chamaeleontidae
LIFESTYLE: Arboreal; forest
DIET: Insectivorous
AVERAGE LENGTH: 10 inches (25 cm)

*Horned mountain dragon (*Acanthosaura crucigera*). Some of these lizards live underneath fallen leaves.*

NATIVE CLIMATE: Savannah, tropical rain forest

NATURAL DISTRIBUTION: Africa

True chameleons are among the most fascinating of all lizards. Three rigid horns are present on the male of this species; one horn projecting from the nose, the other two positioned between the eyes on the forehead. Both sexes of this species have prehensile tails and powerful, interestingly engineered toes that they use for clutching and climbing branches. Insects that come into view of this lizard's pivoting eyes often find

A female Jackson's chameleon (Chamaeleo jacksonii). *Members of this species have been known to breed in captivity.*

The knight anole *(Anolis equestris), like other anole species, rarely lives longer than three years.*

themselves no match for the quickness and accuracy of the chameleon's long, projectile tongue. This lizard's ability to change color is similar to that of the green anole (*Anolis carolinensis*). Chameleons do not adjust well to captivity and therefore have short captive lifespans.

Knight Anole (*Anolis equestris*)
FAMILY: Iguanidae
LIFESTYLE: Arboreal; forest
DIET: Insectivorous and carnivorous
AVERAGE LENGTH: 15 inches (38 cm)

NATIVE CLIMATE: Savannah
NATURAL DISTRIBUTION: Cuba; introduced into Florida

In shape and behavior this anole closely resembles the green anole (*Anolis carolinensis*), although the adult knight anole is approximately three times larger when fully grown.

Madagascar Day Gecko (*Phelsuma madagascariensis*)
FAMILY: Gekkonidae
LIFESTYLE: Arboreal; forest
DIET: Omnivorous
AVERAGE LENGTH: 10 inches (25 cm)

NATIVE CLIMATE: Tropical rain forest
NATURAL DISTRIBUTION: Madagascar
  This brilliant green gecko is diurnal (active by day). This species is found only on the island of Madagascar off the southeastern coast of Africa. Red markings on the back and head give this lizard a striking color pattern. *Phelsuma cepediana*, another day gecko that resembles the Madagascar day gecko, is indigenous only to the island of Mauritius in the Indian Ocean near Madagascar.

Northern Curly-tailed Lizard (*Leiocephalus carinatus*)
FAMILY: Iguanidae
LIFESTYLE: Arboreal/somewhat terrestrial; forest/also rocky areas and cliffs
DIET: Mainly insectivorous
AVERAGE LENGTH: 13 inches (33 cm)
NATIVE CLIMATE: Savannah
NATURAL DISTRIBUTION: West Indies, introduced to the Florida Keys
  This species of curly-tailed lizard usually can be kept in a tropical environment. It is hardy and inexpensive.

*Below and opposite: Madagascar day geckos (*Phelsuma madagascariensis*) must be provided with plenty of water and ample opportunities to sunbathe.*

Tokay Gecko (*Gekko gecko*)
FAMILY: Gekkonidae
LIFESTYLE: Arboreal, forest; also rocky areas and cliffs
DIET: Insectivorous and carnivorous
AVERAGE LENGTH: 12 inches (30 cm)
NATIVE CLIMATE: Savannah, tropical rain forest
NATURAL DISTRIBUTION: Southeast Asia

This nocturnal (active at night) gecko has a bark and a bite. The voice of this species can be heard clearly, and the lizard seldom hesitates biting its keeper at the slightest provocation. The large, cat-like eyes lack movable eyelids; and (like many other geckos) these lizards clear their eyes with the use of their tongues. Tokay geckos are somewhat

A pair of northern curly-tailed lizards (Leiocephalus carinatus). This species is known for its very large scales.

*The tokay gecko (*Gekko gecko*) needs rocks and branches for climbing and should be kept in a terrarium with high humidity.*

useful as in-house exterminators of certain unwanted insects. Insects that are contaminated with pesticides, however, will most likely prove to be lethal to the lizards. Toe pads that enable these lizards to climb up walls and along ceilings enhance this gecko's ability at insect control.

Iguana Primer

This special section on *Iguana iguana* has been included as a result of the sustained interest in this lizard by pet keepers. Some of the information that follows can be applied to other species of tropical lizards as well as to certain species of large non-tropical lizards. Other data, such as the suggested diet, obviously apply only to *Iguana*.

The juvenile iguana is mainly insectivorous. Its diet in captivity consists chiefly of insects such as mealworms and crickets, although vegetables and fruits are often accepted. Although the adult iguana is mainly a herbivore, it sometimes accepts poultry, fish, and beef. Insects are rarely consumed by the adult iguana.

It is a misconception that the iguana can thrive on a diet of lettuce, tomatoes, and mealworms. To ensure that the iguana's appetite remains sparked, it is important that the lizard's menu be diversified from day to day. The author has observed that many iguanas prefer the following foods: green, yellow, kidney, and baked beans; collard greens; grated carrots; cabbage; melons; apples; bananas; mealworms (for

juvenile iguanas); cheese; and bread. Most canned fruits and vegetables should be washed prior to feeding.

The individual dietary preferences of iguanas vary. The favorite food of one specimen might be an item that is unpalatable to another. Foods that are sometimes accepted by iguanas include: fresh spinach; lima beans; peas; cucumbers; broccoli and broccoli leaves; sweet green peppers; tomatoes; celery and celery leaves; red radishes; lettuce; apricots; peaches; pears; chicken; turkey; tuna; and flowers of the forsythia shrub.

The iguana is rarely observed to eat fruits that contain large amounts of citric acid. These include lemons, limes, oranges, and grapefruits.

The foods listed here represent only a suggested point from which to start when trying to determine the foods that will be the most eagerly accepted. A balanced and varied diet should be an achievable goal if the time and patience required are expended. To ensure that the iguana is receiving adequate nutrition, a suitable vitamin and mineral supplement might be

*The common green iguana (*Iguana iguana*) is a notorious escape artist that must be kept under constant surveillance when taken outdoors.*

added to its food or administered via an eyedropper on a regular basis, paying careful attention to correct dosage. A vitamin and mineral supplement formulated especially for lizards should be available at pet stores that sell reptiles.

The iguana usually can be fed by hand, but the consistency of many foods renders the use of a feeding bowl more appropriate much of the time. The bowl should be large enough to allow the iguana easy access to the food. A constant food source should be available to the lizard, realizing that the animal is inclined to be a forager by nature. This suggests that its digestive system would be better served if the lizard were to ingest small amounts of food throughout the day rather than being compelled to consume all of the nourishment that it requires in one meal.

The iguana drinks water often, usually two or more times a day. Low humidity in the iguana's surroundings will probably make itself evident by the lizard's increased intake of water. Spraying water on the leaves of plants in the iguana's terrarium as a means of attempting to furnish an adequate supply of water for this lizard will fall far short of the intended goal. The iguana should always be provided with a water bowl that should be thoroughly cleaned and refilled daily. The habitat might include an additional container of water in which the iguana can soak its entire body and tail. If the size of the environment permits it, the iguana might be allotted a body of water in which it can swim. A hatchling iguana, which measures close to 8 inches (20 cm) in length, can usually be expected to grow approximately 1 to 1½ inches (2.5–3.8 cm) per month for the first year or two. After the second year the rate of growth declines to an average of much less than 1 inch (2.5 cm) each month. A fully grown iguana might reach a maximum length of around 6½ feet (203 cm), although 5 feet (152 cm) is probably more typical of the size attained by many specimens during a lifespan that plausibly ranges from ten to 25 years.

The iguana has the inborn ability to release a portion of its tail. This seems to occur when the lizard is confronted with a situation that it perceives as

The pet iguana should always be provided with separate water dishes—one for drinking and one for bathing.

being otherwise inescapable. A 22-inch (56 cm) iguana that the author once kept had the misfortune of falling a distance of 6 feet (183 cm) and dropping into a cardboard box. The panicked lizard jumped out of the box leaving 9½ inches (23 cm) of its tail behind. Although bewildered and frightened, the iguana quickly recovered its composure. The bleeding was minimal at the point of separation. The abandoned tail wriggled for a few minutes as though it had a life of its own. After the incident the lizard continued to grow at about the same rate. The tail, however, increased in length only about 1 inch (2.5 cm) from the point where it broke. The section that did grow back was dark brown in color.

Iguanas appear to be much more secure when they are perched near or on the highest peak in their captive surroundings. Much of their time is spent atop the branch that is closest to the ceiling of their terrarium. When permitted to roam throughout the house, the available "crawlspace" at the top of the inside windows is usually preferred by these lizards. A

Be sure to give your iguana the opportunity to exercise, as sedentary pets tend to become obese.

shelf that runs parallel to a windowsill might be constructed. This affords the iguana the option of basking in the sunshine that radiates from outside.

When observing the view from a first-floor window, an iguana's keen eyes are alert to the movement of dogs, cats, and other small animals. The lizard's reactions range from fear to indignation. When forced into a life-threatening confrontation with another animal, an iguana would probably be more successful at convincing its adversary (with the use of a somewhat exaggerated display of its potential viciousness) that it is capable of inflicting serious injury (thus causing the antagonist to flee) than it would be in an attempt to be victorious in battle.

When outraged, an iguana will puff out its body and stand erect on all four legs, giving the impression that the lizard is larger in size than it is in actuality. Dewlapping, an interesting instinctive behavior of many lizards, is usually incorporated into this aggressive performance. A dewlap is the portion of skin located directly below the lizard's chin; it extends from there to the top of its chest region. Dewlapping is the repeated up and down movement of the lizard's head with the dewlap fully extended.

With its mouth half open, the iguana emits a hissing sound that seems to originate from deep within its oral cavity. To convey yet further hostility the lizard moves its tail slowly back and forth, resembling the movement of a snake and suggesting the idea that it is about to strike out with this weaponry. Although lacking prehensile capabilities in its tail, the iguana is endowed with voluntary control over the movement of almost the entire length of its tail. This last threatening display can be more than mere show. An adult iguana can induce pain with a forceful snap of its tail.

The iguana has many small teeth. When the iguana bites, it sometimes clamps its jaws shut and shakes its head back and forth, similar to a dog tugging on a towel when playing with its master.

Judging from the fierce behavior that the irate iguana exhibits, it might seem that its proficiency in the art of self-defense would render it invulnerable to many predators. The truth, however, is that an iguana probably would be defeated in a conflict with any but the smallest of warm-blooded animals.

An unusual and sometimes exasperating behavior that appears to be unrelated to the iguana's display of aggression is this lizard's ability to emit a spray of a salty liquid from its nostrils. This spray may be inadvertently directed onto the iguana keeper's face when feeding or otherwise tending to the lizard.

In captivity the iguana is a territorial reptile. A male specimen does not allow intruders of the same sex within his boundaries. If two adult males are forced to co-exist, one probably will become dominant and harass the passive lizard with frequent hissing and biting. An iguana defending its territory sometimes rams the trespasser with its snout and bites on impact.

It is reasonably safe to assume that a male and female of similar size can be kept as a pair without incident. The females of the species appear to be more passive, which suggests that two or more females might feasibly be housed safely within the same residence. Collectively housing as many as a dozen hatchlings harmoniously is possible, providing that the lizards have sufficient space in which to move about freely. When the hatchlings reach maturity, however (within two to three years), the aggressive individuals might have to be moved to another location if their habitat is too small to accommodate the dominant lizards with the territories they demand.

Large, mature iguanas will sometimes tolerate the presence of hatchlings, although this type of situation should be closely supervised to ensure the safety of the small specimens. An iguana that measures 4 to 5 feet (122–152 cm) in length is equipped with a mouth that is large enough to enable the lizard to swallow a hatchling. Although the probability of this event occurring is questionable, the threat remains that the larger iguana could severely injure or even kill the hatchling with one bite.

The privilege of free reign within the owner's dwelling is best awarded to larger specimens. If man is to coexist comfortably with these reptiles, certain factors must be taken into consideration. The lizard must have a designated place to defecate. A large litter box might be used for this purpose.

The iguana tends to be a creature of habit in regard to this bodily function, although it does sometimes deviate from its usual pattern. A feeding and watering station is necessary. Fresh food and water should be offered daily in sturdy containers.

There are drawbacks to the situation of allowing an iguana to have the run of the house. The potential damage to household items should be taken into consideration. These lizards, when active, represent a possible threat to most breakable articles that are kept within the animal's range. These articles, as well as items that might be possible safety hazards to the iguana itself, should be removed from its surroundings.

An aggravating situation that arises from the presence of a household iguana is the persistence of shed lizard skin that becomes scattered throughout the house as a result of the iguana's molting. The iguana sheds its skin slowly and is almost always in a partial state of molting.

The iguana's natural habitat is, of course, the outdoors. However, a large lizard that allows its owner to fasten a leash to its body and calmly

The mouth of an adult iguana is large enough to hold a young member of its own species or a smaller lizard. Be sure your iguana's cagemates are of a comparable size.

consents to a leisurely stroll outside is a rare commodity. The keeper might be scratched or bitten as a result of the specimen's reluctance to accept the restraint exacted upon its movement by a harness. Gloves should be worn when handling an uncooperative lizard. (Iguanas, as well as all lizards, should be handled as infrequently as possible. Severe damage to the lizard can result if its tail is used as a means of

manipulating the lizard.)

An appropriate type of restraining device that can be employed on the common green iguana as well as other large lizards, if the lizard will tolerate its application, is a nylon harness and leash intended for use on cats and small dogs. This unit, which is one continuous piece, is comprised of two adjustable loops that lead into a leash. The front loop is placed over the lizard's head and should be positioned behind the iguana's dewlap. Care should be taken to avoid damaging the bony structure inside the dewlap. The loose strap that remains is looped around the lizard's chest behind its front legs and is fastened to the top of the harness. Avoid an unnecessary degree of tightness, which can choke and/or pinch the lizard.

Difficulties can arise with the "domesticated" iguana when the lizard is taken outside. The iguana seems insecure when outdoors unless it is perched in a tree. On a level, grassy area an iguana usually flattens itself out on the ground, probably in an attempt to conceal itself from predators. If the iguana is permitted to settle down on a tree limb the leash can be tied to a branch and the lizard can be allowed to have some time to itself, although close observation should be maintained to prevent any hazardous situations from developing.

As practical and convenient as is this harness, the iguana can be fairly adept at wriggling out of it. Other potential sources of danger to the iguana that is tethered to a tree include cats, dogs, wild animals, and inquisitive children.

Iguana wearing a leash. More and more hobbyists are finding that leashes help to keep their evasive iguanas in check.

An alternative to taking the iguana outdoors on a leash is an outdoor cage. A simple structure can be constructed using wood and wire screening. This temporary shelter can be used on warm, sunny days. The cage should always provide the availability of shade, as should any environment in which an iguana is housed. Branches for climbing and food and water also should be at the iguana's disposal within the cage. Leaving the cage unattended while the lizard is occupying it should be avoided for obvious reasons.

A problem that might occur with the use of this type of cage is the possibility that the iguana will injure itself while trying to escape through the wire screening. Another factor that might be relevant to this situation involves the digging capabilities of these lizards. Remember that the female iguana deposits her eggs in burrows that she digs in the earth. Proficiency at this endeavor might enable the lizard to dig a large enough tunnel under the cage to escape through if the ground is used for the floor of the makeshift cage.

The common green iguana

Large iguanas are capable of digging a tunnel under an outdoor cage in order to escape.

is a tropical lizard that hails from a warm, humid climate. Owners of these lizards who allow the animals to have the run of the house rather than providing them with a tropical terrarium might aid their pets by occasionally spraying them lightly with water. This is especially important to the keeper who lives in an area where the climate is temperate or cooler, because winter months are considerably drier in these locations. Spraying should of course be done inside the warmth of the house. Tropical lizards should never be taken outside if the temperature is below 70°F (21°C).

Steppe and Desert Zones

STEPPE CLIMATE

The dry climates of the world are divided into two major categories—steppe (semi-arid) and desert (arid). Both of these climates have an average relative humidity factor of 12 to 30% during the middle of the day, but average annual precipitation of steppe climates is 10 to 20 inches (25–50 cm), while desert precipitation usually averages below 10 inches (25 cm) annually. Certain steppes and deserts are tropical. Other semi-arid and arid climates exhibit a winter season that resembles the climatic conditions that exist in certain temperate

*A chuckwalla (*Sauromalus obesus*). Members of this species love to eat plant blossoms.*

*A sun-gazer (*Cordylus giganteus*). For the most part, members of the genus* Cordylus *adapt well to captivity and make good pets.*

zones during the winter.

"Cool" steppes have a true winter season. Temperatures in these areas during the winter months can fall to $-30°F$ ($-35°C$). The distinguishing factors between steppe regions and areas that are truly temperate in climate are the low amount of rainfall and the correspondingly low relative humidity that is present in the steppes. Conversely, temperate climates receive much more annual rainfall and are influenced by high relative humidity during the summer months.

The "cool" steppes, which are predominantly located within the middle latitudes, mirror the climate of tropical steppes only during summer months that yield high maximum temperatures. Areas where "cool" steppe climates can be found are as follows: much of the western United States (westward from approximately 100°W longitude); approximately half of northern Mexico; a section of southern Argentina; and part of eastern Australia.

"Hot" tropical steppes, which are primarily found in the low latitudes, maintain a mean annual temperature of at least 70°F (21°C). Average temperatures during the hottest month range from the low 80s to 95°F (27–35°C). Maximum highs at this period are often 100 to 120°F (38–50°C); nighttime temperatures average 70 to 80°F (21–27°C). During the coolest months high temperatures are approximately 50 to 70°F (10–21°C); lows average between 30 to 40°F (−2–5°C). A mild frost is possible during this cooler season.

"Hot" tropical steppes are found in: sections of the interior of Mexico; a few relatively small areas of South America; much of southern Africa; part of eastern Africa; the African Sudan; and a large section of northern Australia.

*The collared lizard (*Crotaphytus collaris*) is equipped with powerful hindlegs, making it an excellent jumper.*

*A banded gecko (*Coleonyx variegatus*). This species often takes a hibernation hiatus if its conditions are too cold.*

DESERT CLIMATE

Desert climates, like steppe climates, can be divided into two classes. "Hot" tropical deserts are primarily of low latitude location; "cool" deserts are mainly found between the middle latitudes. "Cool" deserts are not the same as "cold" deserts. Expanses of arctic tundra, which are true deserts, are referred to as "cold" deserts. These tundra deserts are not of concern in this book.

"Cool" deserts register maximum summer temperatures of 100 to 110°F (38–43°C); summer nighttime low temperatures of 40°F (5°C) are possible. The "cool" desert, which has a true winter season, often experiences temperatures that are below the freezing mark during this period.

Although relative humidity probably averages approximately 20% throughout the daylight hours, it is quite possible for the humidity factor to reach 100% at night. Regions affected by a "cool"

*Savannah monitor (*Varanus exanthematicus*). This species tolerates large fluctuations in temperature.*

desert climate include the following: parts of the Great Basin of the United States as well as the Sonoran and Chihuahuan Deserts of the U.S., the interior of northern Mexico, and a large portion of southeastern Argentina.

"Hot" tropical deserts maintain the record of the highest temperature ever recorded—136.4°F (58°C) in the shade at Azizia, Libya (Sahara Desert). The highest recorded temperature in the United States is 134°F (57°C) at Death Valley.

The mean annual temperature and the average monthly high and low temperatures of tropical deserts are nearly the same as those of the "hot" tropical steppe climate. However, the maximum high temperatures achieved in the desert regions are greater. Extreme highs of 120°F (50°C), as well as low temperatures near 32°F (0°C) are common.

Locations of tropical deserts are as follows: most of the Mojave Desert of the United States; the Baja Peninsula; a small section of northwestern Mexico; the African Sahara Desert; much of the Kalahari Desert of Africa; Australia's Great Sandy Desert; and parts of the eastern coast of South America, as well as a relatively small section of the eastern interior of Argentina.

CLIMATE AND ENVIRONMENT

Lizards that originate from steppe or desert climates usually can be housed within the same type of terrarium environment. Daytime temperatures are probably most appropriate when maintained between 80 and 100°F (27–38°C). Nighttime lows should most likely be kept at or above 68 to 70°F (20–21°C). Low humidity is a factor that might be difficult to provide, especially if the owner of a dry-climate lizard lives in a tropical or subtropical climate zone. It seems best that a daytime relative humidity factor of 20% or less should be the intended goal.

Desert iguana (Dipsosaurus dorsalis). This species is incapable of digesting its food when the temperature drops below 90°F (32°C).

Although these lizards are indigenous to climates that exhibit extremely high temperatures, it should be realized that they cannot withstand severe heat if exposed to its full intensity.

Many desert lizards are most active during the late morning and early evening hours when the heat of the day is not as excessive. Although certain species of desert lizards can tolerate air temperatures that are near 110°F (43°C), it is totally impossible for these reptiles to survive noontime surface temperatures in these regions, which might reach as high as 200°F (93°C). These lizards must take refuge from the intense heat of the midday and early afternoon sun. To safely regulate its body temperature a desert lizard will find a location where water or shade is available, or it might burrow into cooler sand or soil. The desert terrarium should offer all of these possible alternatives to the lizards. Lizards are able to pant when the surrounding temperature becomes too hot. This action helps to lower their body temperatures. If a captive desert lizard is observed to pant while in a shaded location of the terrarium, it should be a clear indication that the

A member of the genus Varanus. *If your lizard's terrarium is equipped with a light bulb for warmth, be sure to provide an area of shelter.*

*A variegated monitor (*Varanus varius*). Members of this species are ground-dwellers.*

temperature in the environment is excessively high.

Before night falls many diurnal lizards bury themselves in the warm desert sand or otherwise secure a warm, sheltered area for themselves. To provide captive lizards with the option of burrowing, a suitable depth of "loose" substrate should be applied to the floor of the terrarium. Aquarium sand or gravel apportioned at the rate of 3 inches (7.5 cm) of substrate to 1 inch (2.5 cm) of the lizard's height is probably the minimum practical depth that can be used. Sandy soil also

can be used as a substrate in the desert habitat.

Heating the substrate of the desert terrarium can be accomplished with the use of heating cables or pads that are designed specifically for such applications. With safety in mind, always be certain that the heating appliance is waterproof and that it is suitable for subterranean use. Standard heating pads designed to afford comfort to humans are not safe to use in the terrarium situation. If an under-substrate heater is incorporated into the desert environment, the electrical wiring should be kept dry and should be inaccessible to the lizards.

It should be remembered that the presence of water in any terrarium will increase the relative humidity factor. It is probably best to use a simple water bowl in the desert habitat. The use of a drip system, waterfall, or airstone, all of which create excessive humidity, should be avoided. The water bowl should be shallow, but large enough to accommodate the lizard's entire body and tail; the lizard might opt to soak in the water as well as to drink it. With a little creative rockwork the water bowl can be concealed, simulating a natural water hole. Easy access both in and out of the water should be provided; not all lizards are good swimmers. Any rocks placed in the water should be non-sedimentary, such as shale and other rocks that are safe for use in freshwater aquaria.

Most of the other usual terrarium decor items, such as driftwood, can be used to enhance the rustic environment. Depending upon the species of lizard that is being housed in the terrarium, cliffs and rocky areas or a more open setting can be arranged. In terraria of all climate types it is important to arrange the decor in a fashion that will negate the chance of possible injury to the inhabitants that might be caused by unstable rocks, logs, and other scenery. The substrate in all lizard terraria must be replaced occasionally to maintain cleanliness of the environment. Additionally, when live plants are added to the lizard's terrarium it is best to be aware of the potential danger of the pesticides and fertilizers that might be harbored on or in the plants. The desert terrarium, as well as all lizard habitats, is probably best kept on a daily schedule of 12 to 16 hours of light.

There is a large variety of live plants that might be successfully maintained in the confines of a desert terrarium. Cacti and succulent plants that require a humidity factor of 50% or less are probably the best candidates for this type of habitat.

Haworthia (wart plant), a succulent plant, might be a good choice to include in a desert terrarium. However, this plant, as well as most plants that require a dry environment, might not survive unless

*A snake-eyed lizard (*Ophisops elegans*). Snake-eyes are delicate lizards that generally are unfit for keeping in captivity.*

provided with the proper conditions all year. Most "desert" plants, including cacti, must be allowed to remain dry and cool during the winter months when the plants become dormant. The amount of watering needed varies with the different species.

Another concern when deciding which live plants to choose for inclusion in the

A collared lizard (Crotaphytus collaris) taking a drink. Collared lizards require a well-defined daily temperature cycle.

desert terrarium is the type of spine present on various species of cactus. Groups of small, easily detachable spines are found on many species of cacti. If this type of plant is included in the terrarium it would be best to check the lizard specimens frequently for the presence of spines that might become embedded in their skin. Remove the spines with tweezers. The other kind of cactus needle that might be hazardous to lizards is the extremely sharp, hard, single pin-like spine found on many species of cactus and other succulents. It might be

possible to remove at least the sharp point from the end of the spine (with nail clippers) without damaging the plant.

Many species of the cactus genus *Cereus* are hardy plants that can withstand the rigors of terrarium life. The cactus genus *Parodia* offers another choice. Both of these cacti require low humidity. Several genera of cacti that are best kept at a slightly higher relative humidity level include *Espostoa*, *Opuntia*, and *Pachypodium*. *Espostoa* species can be kept warm most of the year. *Pachypodium* species resemble foliage plants until the leaves drop off at a certain time of the year to expose a cactus-like body. These three cacti should be maintained at a relative humidity factor of 50 to 60%.

Sansaveria (mother-in-law's tongue) is a very hardy plant that can tolerate extremely harsh environmental conditions. Although *Sansaveria* is a foliage plant, its ability to adapt itself to severe circumstances might render this plant the distinction of being the most suitable plant for any type of terrarium environment.

All of the desert plants that have been mentioned require full direct sunlight. The succulent plant *Haworthia* requires low relative humidity. *Sansaveria* also can be considered as a plant that requires a low level of humidity, but the truth actually is that the plant is so hardy that it will simply tolerate the lack of moisture in the air.

It is best to allow the plants to remain in individual pots whether a cage with a false bottom or an all-glass aquarium is used. Plants as well as lizards demand certain environmental requirements if they are to be maintained in good health. It is sometimes difficult to juggle these prerequisites in order of importance and arrive at a

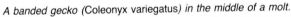

A banded gecko *(Coleonyx variegatus)* in the middle of a molt.

compromise that is acceptable to both the plants and animals that inhabit the terrarium. Trial and error, under these circumstances, seems inevitable.

STEPPE AND DESERT LIZARDS
Armadillo Lizard (*Cordylus cataphractus*)
FAMILY: Cordylidae
LIFESTYLE: Terrestrial, field-oriented; rocky areas and cliffs
DIET: Insectivorous
AVERAGE LENGTH: 7 inches (18 cm)
NATIVE CLIMATE: Tropical steppe and desert
NATURAL DISTRIBUTION: South Africa

These tough-scaled lizards usually can be maintained peacefully with several members of their own species. The armadillo lizard belongs to

Armadillo lizards (Cordylus cataphractus) were named for their tendency to curl up when threatened.

A leopard gecko (Eublepharis macularius). Members of this genus are also known as fat-tailed geckos.

the minority of lizards which are live-bearers.

Banded Gecko (*Coleonyx variegatus*)

FAMILY: Gekkonidae
LIFESTYLE: Terrestrial, field-oriented; rocky areas
DIET: Insectivorous
AVERAGE LENGTH: 5 inches (12.5 cm)
NATIVE CLIMATE: Cool steppe and desert, tropical desert
NATURAL DISTRIBUTION: Southwestern North America

This small nocturnal gecko, unlike many species of the family, has true eyelids.

Moreover, the banded gecko lacks the toe pads that enable many geckos to climb vertically on flat surfaces.

Chuckwalla (*Sauromalus obesus*)
FAMILY: Iguanidae
LIFESTYLE: Terrestrial, field-oriented; rocky areas
DIET: Mainly herbivorous, but somewhat insectivorous
AVERAGE LENGTH: 15 inches (37.5 cm)
NATIVE CLIMATE: Cool desert, tropical desert
NATURAL DISTRIBUTION: Western North America

Unlike most desert lizards, the chuckwalla is almost completely herbivorous. The fruit of the prickly pear cactus is preferred by these somewhat husky iguanids, although they do ingest other species of desert flowers, leaves, and fruits. Infrequently, they consume insects.

Collared Lizard (*Crotaphytus collaris*)
FAMILY: Iguanidae
LIFESTYLE: Terrestrial, field-oriented; rocky areas
DIET: Insectivorous; carnivorous
AVERAGE LENGTH: 12 inches (30 cm)
NATIVE CLIMATE: Cool steppe, cool desert, tropical desert

A pair of chuckwallas (Sauromalus obesus). Chuckwallas are completely herbivorous; one of the strange quirks of their diet is the fact that they will eat the fruit of the prickly pear cactus.

*A female Texas horned lizard (*Phrynosoma cornutum*) just after squirting blood from her eye; the stream of blood can be projected up to seven feet.*

NATURAL DISTRIBUTION: Western North America

This active, aggressive species is capable of running on its hind legs. Its captive life span is relatively long when the lizard is properly cared for.

Desert Iguana (*Dipsosaurus dorsalis*)

FAMILY: Iguanidae
LIFESTYLE: Terrestrial, field-oriented; mostly open areas, also rocky areas
DIET: Mainly herbivorous, somewhat insectivorous
AVERAGE LENGTH: 15 inches (37.5 cm)

NATIVE CLIMATE: Cool desert, tropical desert
NATURAL DISTRIBUTION: Western North America

The diet of this lizard is similar to that of the chuckwalla. Desert iguanas are incapable of digesting food when the surrounding temperature is lower than 90°F (32°C).

Texas Horned Lizard (*Phrynosoma cornutum*)

FAMILY: Iguanidae
LIFESTYLE: Terrestrial, field-oriented; open and rocky areas
DIET: Ants (almost exclusively);

sometimes eats other insects

AVERAGE LENGTH: 6½ inches (16 cm)

NATIVE CLIMATE: Cool steppe, cool desert

NATURAL DISTRIBUTION: Southwestern U.S. and northern Mexico

When antagonized this species of horned lizard is able to emit a fine stream of blood from its eyes; the blood can be projected up to 7 feet (2.1 m).

This lizard can also puff out its body by filling itself with air. Such extreme defense mechanisms are necessary because the horned lizard, sometimes referred to as the "horned toad," is a relatively small, non-aggressive lizard. The health of these lizards usually deteriorates quickly when the animals are kept in captivity due to difficult temperature and humidity

*A Mexican horned lizard (*Phrynosoma asio*).*

*Warren's girdled lizard (*Cordylus warreni*). If possible, this species should be maintained in an outdoor terrarium during warm months.*

requirements and the inability of the keeper to provide the horned lizards with their specialized diet of ants. It would be interesting to discover if a keeper of these lizards has ever attempted to establish an "ant farm" in a terrarium prior to the introduction of the horned toad to the environment. Sale and collection of *Phrynosoma* species is now greatly restricted by law in many areas. These are delicate lizards that should not be kept by inexperienced hobbyists even if available.

*A leopard lizard (*Gambelia wislizenii*).*

Leopard Lizard (*Gambelia wislizenii*)
FAMILY: Iguanidae
LIFESTYLE: Terrestrial, field-oriented; mostly open areas, also rocky areas
DIET: Omnivorous
AVERAGE LENGTH: 13½ inches (32 cm)
NATIVE CLIMATE: Cool steppe, cool desert, tropical desert
NATURAL DISTRIBUTION: Western North America

This species exhibits many aspects of behavior that parallel those of the collared lizard, but the leopard lizard is probably more inclined to accept certain flowers and plant material as part of its diet.

Savannah Monitor (*Varanus exanthematicus*)
FAMILY: Varanidae
LIFESTYLE: Terrestrial, field-oriented; open and rocky areas
DIET: Mainly carnivorous, also insectivorous
AVERAGE LENGTH: 4½ feet (1.4 cm)

NATIVE CLIMATE: Tropical steppe, tropical desert
NATURAL DISTRIBUTION: Africa (south of the Sahara Desert)

If the humidity is kept low, plenty of sunshine is provided, and the correct diet is fed to this lizard, it should prove to be very hardy.

Side-blotched Lizard (*Uta stansburiana*)

FAMILY: Iguanidae
LIFESTYLE: Terrestrial, field-oriented; mostly rocky areas, also open areas
DIET: Insectivorous
AVERAGE LENGTH: 5 inches (12.5 cm)

NATIVE CLIMATE: Cool steppe, tropical steppe, cool desert, tropical desert
NATURAL DISTRIBUTION: Western U.S. and Mexico

Many animals that are indigenous to the North American West include these lizards as part of their natural diet. Due to their small size, these lizards represent an opportunity for the amateur herpetologist to establish a moderate-sized, less expensive desert or steppe terrarium. However, these lizards as well as lizards of all species should not be housed in cramped quarters.

*Savannah monitor (*Varanus exanthematicus*). Monitors have painful bites; therefore, they must be handled with extreme care.*

Recruiting the Perfect Specimen

Possible mishandling of a lizard during capture or shipping can result in injuries to the specimen that might render it an unlikely candidate for survival in captivity. Even when the lizard arrives in good condition, the health of a specimen can deteriorate rapidly if cared for improperly.

As with any purchase, especially one that involves the investment of human emotions, it is usually the best policy to shop around before committing to a transaction. Starting out with a vigorous, disease-free lizard should increase the margin of success that the owner will experience in an attempt to provide the specimen with a long, healthy life.

Common sense should provide the necessary guidelines for evaluation of the overall appearance and attitude of a lizard. A healthy, content specimen should be somewhat active and should exhibit an interest in food. An even pattern of coloration should be evident. A lizard that appears drab in color still might be in sound health—when certain species that are capable of color changes alter their pigmentation toward the darker end of the spectrum

available to them, it is an indication that the animals are feeling disturbed or threatened. For many lizards, especially adult specimens that have recently been removed from their natural habitat, the displaying of this reaction in captivity usually can be considered normal.

More specifically, the lizard should be checked for signs of dehydration, malnutrition, mouth rot, and broken bones (including the tail). Further inspection of the animal might reveal ticks, cuts, tumors, or abrasions. The lizard's belly should be examined for the presence of ulcerations on its scales that might have been caused by overexposure to a wet or very damp surface for an extended period of time.

If incorrect environmental conditions and/or inappropriate diet is all that is available, most species of lizards virtually waste away. After a certain point of neglect it is extremely

Opposite: *A common tegu (Tupinambis teguixin). Before purchasing any lizard, be sure to check it thoroughly for mites and ticks.*

difficult for most lizards to recover, even when pampered. It is sometimes possible, however, to nurture an inadequately cared for specimen back to health. If this is accomplished, it is its own reward.

When the healthiest available specimen is located, the price of the lizard has to be reckoned with. As the demand for an animal increases, it appears that the retail cost simultaneously rises, much to the disappointment of many consumers. Perhaps some good might be derived from this price hike. The type of individual who might buy an animal on a whim and later decide that the pet has outlived its novelty will think twice before spending such an amount of money on a lizard. Prices vary drastically depending upon the species of lizard and its availability. The green anole (*Anolis carolinensis*) might be purchased for as little as 2–5% of the cost of a more exotic species such as some monitor lizards.

Once purchased, very little should be anticipated in regard to the relationship between a lizard and its keeper. Certain species of freshwater tropical and marine fish, unlike many lizards, are more apt to interact with their owners.

COMPATIBILITY

Several factors should be considered when planning which domestic pets might be allowed to interact with lizards. Most cats and dogs will kill and possibly eat a lizard that is incapable of successfully defending itself. Large lizards such as monitors might kill and possibly eat cats and dogs. Certain birds eat lizards. Conversely, certain lizards will eat birds as well as devour many varieties of small mammals on instinct, including mice, rats, and hamsters. The possibility exists that compatibility among some of these animals might be attainable, although it should never be taken for granted.

The three major concerns regarding compatibility among various specimens of lizards are sex, degree of territorial behavior exhibited by the individual species, and the size of the lizards that you can hope will coexist in peace. Individual situations might be exempt from these determining criteria, however, so it is best to proceed with caution when integrating various specimens

A male helmeted iguana (Corytophanes cristatus) should never be kept with another male of its species.

into a community lizard environment.

An attempt to peacefully maintain two or more mature adult male lizards of the same species within the same environment probably will result in failure. If these lizards are housed in a very sizable habitat or if they are large specimens that have the run of the house, the chances for success increase. Even under these conditions the lizards might fight fiercely on occasion. Two male specimens of different species might tolerate each other to a much higher degree than is usually the case with two male lizards that belong to the same species. Females of many lizard species tend to be less aggressive, thus they usually

*A green anole (*Anolis carolinensis*) should only be kept with lizards of its own size and temperament.*

can be housed somewhat more peacefully with lizards of either gender as well as with members of related and unrelated lizard species. An important fact to remember when a terrarium is being stocked with lizards is that many large lizards eat small lizards. Small, delicate, soft-skinned lizards—for example, the green anole (*Anolis carolinensis*)—would probably be devoured by most large lizards, regardless of species, if introduced to the larger lizard's environment. Small, tough-skinned lizards, such as the sun-gazers (*Cordylus* spp.), might have a better chance of survival when placed in a terrarium with large lizards, although this is by no means a certainty.

Lizards might peacefully coexist with some animals that are commonly kept in a terrarium situation. Small hermit crabs usually can be housed with large lizards. Large hermit crabs tend to climb over lizards, becoming a source of aggravation and possible injury to the lizards. Certain frogs, newts, and turtles might make compatible terrarium mates for lizards of appropriate size. True compatibility among animals such as these can only be determined by the test of time. Close observation should be maintained when an attempt is made to establish an environment that incorporates various species of animals. Otherwise, the habitat might eventually house only one extremely plump resident.

When housing a combination of different species of animals within the same living quarters, the proper requirements for each animal that inhabits the environment must be met while avoiding the dilution of the needs of any other specimen that occupies the habitat, whether terrarium, aqua-terrarium, or cage. Only species that are native to similar environments should be considered as potential candidates for inclusion in community habitats.

A sun-gazer (Cordylus cordylus). Sun-gazers are small but can hold their own with lizards that are a bit larger.

Nutrition and Health

The quality of nutrition provided to the "domestic" lizard is a crucial determining factor in the successful maintenance of the animal's health. Malnutrition is a serious threat to captive lizards, and a challenge is presented in competently providing these creatures with suitable diets that are sufficient for their individual needs.

Most species of lizards exhibit a preference for at least one of the four basic diets. Herbivorous lizards ingest various forms of vegetation. Certain species prefer leafy foliage that they procure from trees and shrubs, as well as grasses such as wheat. Some lizards are fond of vegetables and/or fruits. The petals, buds, and blossoms of certain flowers are considered food items by many herbivorous lizards. Flower nectar as well as the fruit of a specific cactus is eaten by certain lizards. Honey is accepted by some geckos. There is a wide variety of plant material that might be offered to lizards that exhibit herbivorous appetites.

All food served to herbivorous lizards, whether gathered from the outdoors or purchased in a grocery store, should be thoroughly washed prior to feeding in an effort to eliminate the possibility of presenting the lizards with food that is contaminated with pesticides.

It is probably safe to say that most lizards are at least somewhat insectivorous and that many lizards are entirely insectivorous. Crickets and grasshoppers are insects commonly accepted by insectivorous lizards. The purchase or outdoor collection of these insects appears to be much easier in the long run than attempting to cultivate them.

Crickets are often available at pet stores. Grasshoppers can be collected in many locations during the summer months. Like any other insects, grasshoppers should be taken only from areas that are free from pesticide contamination.

Mealworms are the larval form of *Tenebrio molitor*, a flour beetle. Although the

Crickets can be cultured at home or purchased at a pet shop. Never feed your lizard a wild-caught cricket unless you're sure the insect comes from an uncontaminated area.

pupae and beetles are usually unacceptable to the lizards as food items, the mealworms are often consumed. Mealworms are white just after they shed their tough, chitinous exterior; this is the best time to feed these insect larvae to lizards. If the light brown "hard-shelled" mealworms are used as the main staple of a lizard's diet, the animal will probably experience digestive and intestinal problems that can lead to its demise.

Many insects on which insectivorous lizards will feed can be collected outdoors. Small soft-bodied spiders may be preferred. With the lizard's best interest in mind, large spiders with tough exoskeletons as well as poisonous spiders should be excluded from the animal's diet. In summer, houseflies can be collected during the day and moths might be gathered at night. Avoid caterpillars that have bristles and/or spines; only caterpillars with smooth skin should be offered to lizards.

Earthworms can be collected or purchased for some lizards. If the worms are collected they should be taken only from areas that are ecologically clean, and even then it is best to let them stay on damp paper towels for several hours until they pass their gut contents.

Fruitflies and aphids make suitable insectivorous food for very small lizards as well as for small newborn or hatchling lizards. Aphids usually can be obtained easily in the summertime. When a small branch that contains a cluster of aphids is located, it can be detached from the plant and placed in the lizard's terrarium. When collecting aphids it is best to be aware of the possibility of pesticide contamination to the plant from which the branch is taken.

Fruitflies (*Drosophila*) can be collected or cultured. Winged and wingless varieties are equally suitable as food for lizards. Wingless fruitflies must be obtained from a pet store or a mail order dealer who advertises such commodities. The winged version of the fruitfly can be collected by placing a jar containing a piece of banana on a windowsill

*A giant mealworm beetle (*Coleoptera*). Adult beetles have been known to attack animals they were supposed to feed.*

during the summer and fall.

Carnivorous lizards consume other animals, usually whole. The size of the carnivorous lizard often determines the prey that it devours. If large enough, carnivorous lizards will eat rodents such as mice and rats; other victims of a large lizard's appetite might include chickens, other birds and their eggs, and amphibians such as frogs. Many carnivorous lizards also devour reptiles, including other lizards. Although a few types of small lizards are often sold in pet stores as food for larger lizards, the author does not recommend this practice.

If red meat (such as beef) is substituted for live foods on a continual basis, the lizard receiving this type of diet will develop a calcium deficiency unless an adequate supplement of bone meal is provided. Beef that is fed to lizards should be extremely lean. Pork should never be fed to lizards.

I believe that the use of live mice and rats as lizard food should be avoided. Live rodents can sometimes injure or even kill a lizard before it has a chance to subdue the intended prey. Frozen rodents can be purchased from pet shops and also from mail order dealers.

Omnivorous lizards are

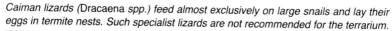

Caiman lizards (Dracaena *spp.) feed almost exclusively on large snails and lay their eggs in termite nests. Such specialist lizards are not recommended for the terrarium.*

*The Nile monitor (*Varanus niloticus*) is a goat among lizards—it will eat almost anything.*

those species that consume animal matter as well as plant material. A lizard that eats plants and insects but does not eat "higher" (i.e. vertebrate) animals can also be classified as an omnivore. As with all lizards, it is essential to provide the omnivorous lizard with a balanced and varied diet. This might be more easily achieved with omnivores than with any other lizards simply because such a variety of foods appeals to them. Adult carnivores that are accustomed to a certain diet in their natural habitat usually are the most difficult lizards to cater to.

Specialized diets are exhibited by certain lizards.

111

*Lilford's wall lizard (*Podarcis lilfordi*). This species is very delicate and does not do well in captivity.*

The caiman lizard (*Dracaena guianensis*) exists on a diet that is almost limited to clams and snails. Horned lizards (*Phrynosoma*) depend almost exclusively on a natural diet of ants. The horned mountain dragons (*Acanthosaura*) and helmeted iguanas (*Corytophanes*) might derive their entire natural nutrition from earthworms and grubs. In contrast, the Nile monitor (*Varanus niloticus*) is a veritable garbage disposal that devours living and dead animals of all kinds, providing the food is not too large.

Regardless of the lizard's dietary preferences, a suitable vitamin supplement as well as bone meal (be certain there are no fertilizer additives) should be administered on a routine basis. Bone meal can be dusted onto or injected into insects and feeder animals before offering them to the lizards. Cultured live foods can be fed a diet that is rich in vitamins and bone meal prior to their being fed to the lizards. Herbivores might receive their supplements in a folded leaf that contains the added nutrients. Monitors and tegus, which are occasionally allowed a meal of red meat and raw eggs, will gobble up the supplements along with the food. Certain individual lizards might even accept their vitamin doses from an eyedropper.

To prevent the occurrence of rickets or softening of the lizard's bones, the animal should be given a diet that provides a satisfactory amount of calcium, and adequate sunshine or its equivalent also should be available to the lizard.

Most lizards can manufacture vitamin D within their bodies when they are exposed to sunlight or a similar light source. When such exposure is limited, the diet of most lizard species should be enhanced with supplements and foods that contain vitamin D. A cure for rickets and softening of the bones can sometimes be effected by restoring the proper environmental conditions in addition to providing abundant sunshine as well as initiating a

*A racerunner (*Cnemidophorus*). Racerunners were probably named for their stream-lined shape.*

diet that contains high levels of calcium and protein.

Ailments and diseases of lizards manifest themselves in many different forms. Bacterial infections as well as fungal and protozoal diseases are possible threats to the lizard's health. Internal parasites, including tapeworms, and external parasites such as ticks and mites can afflict lizards. Leeches, which are also external parasites, might sometimes be found on semi-aquatic lizards.

Most illnesses that lizards might contract should be treated by a qualified veterinarian. First aid applied by the amateur herpetologist usually is best kept to a minimum. Mouth rot, if treated in its first stages with the use of Mercurochrome solution (2%), might be eradicated. Insignificant cuts and wounds should be cleaned with soapy water and Mercurochrome applied. Until the wound heals

*Opposite: A female double-crested basilisk (*Basiliscus plumifrons*) with cage wear on her lower jaw. Injuries such as this should be treated as soon as possible, as infection can quickly set in.*

it should be observed from time to time to ensure that infection does not set in. In applications where Mercurochrome is unsuitable as a treatment, household hydrogen peroxide might be substituted. Mites and ticks as well as leeches usually can be extracted with tweezers; alcohol can then be applied to the locations from which the parasites were dislodged.

Diseases in lizards are sometimes caused by improper nutrition and incorrect environmental conditions. Inappropriate maintenance may include inadequate provision of sunlight or its equivalent, improper temperature and/or humidity factors, insufficient quantity or incorrect types of food, the existence of extreme air currents, and a cage too small to provide adequate space for the normal activities of the lizard.

Malnutrition and dehydration are consequences that must be dealt with if the lizard's need for nutrition are improperly met. Symptoms of avitaminosis and various other diseases of lizards might include inflammation of the skin, mouth and/or eyes; fading of the skin pigmentation; molting difficulties; and rejection of food and/or water. The lizard might also appear listless and display an urge to remain in a secluded area of its environment. Diarrhea or constipation as well as swelling of the lizard's body might also present themselves as symptoms.

When a lizard's health deteriorates to the point where the specimen is incapable of movement it is probably too late for it to be revitalized. It is worth the effort, however, and presumably the next step should be to seek the professional help of a veterinarian.

Many veterinarians are unfamiliar with reptile zoology and the prerequisites for maintaining the health of lizards in captivity. In an attempt to locate a qualified professional in this field, a telephone call to the local zoological society or public zoo, if either of these organizations exists in the

An agamid lizard. After your lizard has molted, check to be sure that all old skin has come off. Pieces that remain after the molt can cause infection and irritation.

A double-banded chameleon (Chamaeleo bitaeniatus). Chameleons reach adult size at six months and sexual maturity at one year.

surrounding area, might be the course of action to take. If an inquiry is directed toward the herpetology department of such an organization, a veterinarian knowledgeable in the area of reptile zoology might be contacted. Certain cities have herpetology clubs that might have access to the same information.

Many lizards that are examined by veterinarians are diagnosed as having avitaminosis as well as possible dehydration. A lizard in this condition usually is given an emergency injection of vitamins and minerals, and additional tonics of these essential nutrients might also be prescribed. A high calorie paste of the type administered to convalescing cats and dogs also might be advised as part of the lizard's treatment.

At the risk of sounding trite, it might be said that in maintaining a lizard's health, an ounce of prevention definitely is worth at least a pound of cure.

Breeding in Captivity

The majority of lizard species are egg-layers. Most lizards, excluding certain geckos, lay their eggs in concealed locations on or in the ground. Some gecko species are apt to lay their eggs above ground level, producing hard-shelled eggs that can stick to trees, walls, rocks, and other surfaces. Lizards that deposit their eggs at ground level or below usually select a shaded site that offers moist conditions. Areas where decaying logs and vegetation are prevalent are considered ideal. The common tegu (*Tupinambis teguixin*) deposits its eggs within termite mounds in its natural environment. Desert lizard species have a much more difficult time procuring a moist location for laying. The eggs of these lizards are often deposited in sandy soil underneath vegetation and/or rocks.

If eggs are obtained from a captive lizard as a result of the lizard mating in its captive environment or by the chance purchase of a gravid female, the eggs can be removed from the terrarium and incubated. A glass jar or other suitable container can be half filled with moist humus, sphagnum moss, vermiculite, sandy soil, and similar materials. The eggs should not be buried, just placed on top of the substrate. The temperature should be kept between 75 and 85°F (24–30°C). Air circulation is necessary to reduce the possibility of mold. The eggs should not be handled unless it is unavoidable. If mold, or other fungi, starts to develop it must be removed from the eggs and from the substrate. The eggs can receive indirect light, but direct light should be avoided. The eggs should not be kept wet and they should not be permitted to dry out, but they should remain moist. It would be best if an area of the lizard's cage provided the natural requirements for egg-laying that each individual species prefers. Otherwise the lizards might withhold their eggs and become eggbound, which could be lethal.

Comparatively few species of lizards are live-bearers. Only two species of the lizards that are outlined in this book can definitely be considered viviparous: Jackson's

chameleon (*Chamaeleo jacksonii*) and the common girdled lizard (*Cordylus cordylus*) are true live-bearers. Live-bearing lizards give birth in one of two ways, the offspring being born either within an embryonic sac or free of and along with the embryonic sac. The offspring of lizards that deliver the young enclosed in embryonic sacs might occasionally need assistance to emerge from the sac. Extreme caution is advised in this situation—only if it is evident that the newborn lizard is incapable of escaping from its embryonic sac is it advisable to intervene.

Newborn lizards should remain inaccessible to their parents. The offspring have no dependency on their parents for survival, and to their adult counterparts the baby lizards probably represent nothing more than a possible meal. The independent, fast-growing offspring should be provided with water droplets and small insects such as fruitflies, newly hatched crickets, and aphids. Herbivorous newborn lizards might be offered small portions of suitable plant material as well as small insects. It might be considered that the health of the newborn lizard probably reflects the health of the lizard

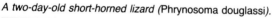

*A two-day-old short-horned lizard (*Phrynosoma douglassi*).*

Chinese water dragons *(Physignathus cocincinus). This species is now being bred in captivity.*

that gave birth to it. With this in mind it seems best to supply a pregnant lizard with a balanced diet that is abundant in calcium as well as in all essential nutrients. Regardless of the care that is invested in accommodating the female lizard with a natural site in which she can deposit her eggs, the eggs might be laid in such obscure locations as on exposed leaves or branches or in water.

It is probably impossible to determine the gender of most newborn lizards, and it remains a difficult task even with juvenile and adult lizards when their outward appearance is used as the basis for judgment. Males usually tend to be larger in size and features as well as being more active and colorful. The most conclusive procedure that can be used to resolve the question of lizard gender is to examine the lizard's cloacal area. Positive identification of male lizards can be made by simultaneously applying light pressure to each side of the lizard's tail base. The cloacal

*A common green iguana (*Iguana iguana*). Determining the gender of a lizard is not easy, but your pet dealer or an experienced hobbyist may be able to help you.*

flap should open somewhat, partially revealing the presence of paired sexual organs (hemipenes) if the specimen is a male lizard; female lizards lack these organs.

If a pair of sexually mature lizards is acquired it is possible that they might attempt to breed in captivity. The author was fortunate enough to witness the mating of a pair of "domestic" common green iguanas. The following account is probably representative of the procedure typical of many tropical and non-tropical lizard species.

When first introduced to the 18-inch (46 cm) female iguana, the male iguana measured 14½ inches (36 cm). These iguanas shared the same habitat for over three years prior to their attempt at reproduction (the common green iguana becomes sexually mature at approximately two to three years of age). With the absence of any type of pairing-off behavior being observed during that time, the mating occurred as somewhat of a surprise.

When the pair began mating the male was 3½ to 4 feet

(107–122 cm) in length; the female, which had previously lost part of its tail, measured only about 3 feet (91 cm) in length although she was slightly wider than the male. The only form of courtship noticed immediately prior to the mating process was a bit of dewlapping performed by the male iguana. The female appeared to display apprehension about the male's intentions.

As the breeding procedure began the male climbed onto the female's back and grasped her tightly with his front and rear legs. The female's movement was then further restricted by the male's intense biting of the skin and/or spines at the top of the female's neck, directly behind her head; the male held the bite until the mating session was completed. When the female was satisfactorily restrained the male forced his tail underneath the female's and completed the mating process. Each time the iguanas mated, the procedure lasted approximately 20 to 30 minutes.

The first day the iguanas were observed to mate was December 13; December 31 was the last day that their mating was observed. Within a span of 17 days the pair was confirmed to have mated at least ten times. The exact days when mating was definitely validated were December 13, 15, 16, 17, 18, 19, 20, 23, 27, and 31.

When the mating season was over it was hoped that the eggs would be laid and that all aspects of the incubation process would conclude with positive results. The female became ill, however, and died a month of so after the mating ceased. Perhaps it would have been best if the pair had only been permitted to mate a few times. They could then have been separated until the mating season drew to a close.

The lack of specific intent directed toward the goal of inducing the iguanas to breed suggests that such positive results are much easier to attain than might otherwise be anticipated. The iguanas were fed an adequate diet and were provided with a satisfactory supply of water. Their cage, which was warmed in the daytime with the use of overhead incandescent light bulbs, was usually regulated by a day/night schedule of approximately 12 hours of light and dark.

Suggested Reading

THE COMPLETELY ILLUSTRATED ATLAS OF REPTILES AND AMPHIBIANS FOR THE TERRARIUM
By Fritz Jurgen Obst, Dr. Klaus Richter, and Dr. Udo Jacob
ISBN 0-86622-958-2
TFH H-1102
Here is a truly comprehensive and beautiful volume covering all reptiles and amphibians any hobbyist (or scientist) is likely to ever see or want to know about. The alphabetical arrangement makes it easy to find information on almost any topic, and the more than 1500 full-color photos make this book a pleasure to look at as well.

BREEDING TERRARIUM ANIMALS
By Elke Zimmermann
ISBN 0-86622-182-4
TFH H-1078
This volume covers everything the hobbyist needs to know about the successful breeding and rearing of terrarium animals, including housing, terrarium, light and heat, breeding food animals, and many other essential topics. In addition to the superlatively informative text, this book contains over 200 full-color and black and white photos.

ALL ABOUT LIZARDS
By Robert Sprackland, Jr.
ISBN 0-87666-764-7
TFH PS-316
For professional and amateur herpetologists and for nature lovers in general, this book contains good advice about keeping lizards in captivity along with excellent taxonomical coverage. In addition, special sections on lizard adaptation, crests and ornamentation, and dangerous lizards are featured. Contains 50 full-color and 78 black and white photos and four line drawings.

LIZARDS IN CAPTIVITY
By Richard H. Wynne
ISBN 0-87666-921-6
TFH PS-769
A useful identification and maintenance guide for amateur and professional herpetologists. Fourteen lizard families are categorized and given complete coverage with regard to distribution, habitat, description, cage requirements, and temperature range. This book is written on a high school level and

contains a glossary of terms, an index of common names, and 58 full-color and 67 black and white photos.

REPTILE DISEASES
By Rolf Hackbarth
ISBN 0-86622-824-1
TFH KW-197
   A no-nonsense look at diseases and health problems of lizards, snakes, and turtles, this volume will prove itself useful to both veterinarian and layman alike. Emphasis is placed upon proper care and on early recognition and treatment of illness. More than 100 full-color photos and drawings supplement the clear and invaluable text, making this book a necessity for anyone interested in reptiles.

*A common tegu (*Tupinambis teguixin*).*

Index

Index

Callopistes maculatus

LIZARDS
KW-196